You Don't Need Headlights to Shine

You Don't Need Headlights to Shine

KATIE RADER

ISBN 979-8-218-59532-6

LCCN: 2024915531

For privacy reasons, some names, locations, and dates may have been changed.

First edition 2024

Typesetting by Roseanna White Designs

Most of the Scripture quotations are from the Authorized (King James) Version. Rights in the Authorized Version in the United Kingdom are vested in the Crown. Reproduced by permission of the Crown's patentee, Cambridge University Press as permission is granted if less than 500 passages and 25% of the total manuscript. Additional Scripture quotations are from the NIV, NIrV, or AMP Bible may be quoted as well, with implied permission as less than 500 verses.

This book is the author's own journal and journey through cancer, and her journey is personal to her, and no two journeys are alike. This book is not intended as a substitute for professional medical advice and not meant to be used, nor should it be used; to diagnose or treat any medical or psychological condition, it is for entertainment purposes only. This book is not intended as a substitute for the medical advice of physicians. The reader should regularly consult a physician in matters relating to their health, particularly with respect to any symptoms that may require diagnosis or medical attention.

Dedication

To all the Survivors, you will never fight alone.
To my Husband and my girls for loving me
through it all +/- boobs.
You are my reason for fighting.
And to my little brother, I love you dearly. Keep fighting.

Table of Contents

Introduction

Let me introduce myself before we get into the cancer stuff. I'm a Floridian, born in Tampa and raised in the country. I married my high school crush, Chad, at 23. I went to cosmetology school while he went to the police academy, and together, we have two incredible daughters, Presley, who was 16 at the time of my diagnosis and Harper, who is 13. We work hard for what we have and live the average American dream.

My grandparents were Christians, and through their faith, my parents became Christians. Through their example, I became one, too. My story didn't start out about sharing my faith. I wanted to update my friends throughout my cancer journey. But Jesus quickly became my main source of survival, so naturally, my story gravitates toward Him. I don't want my faith to deter anyone from reading my story. I have a true relationship with Jesus Christ. Hopefully, my story reaches someone who needs to hear it. I want everyone to see how much Jesus loves us all and I hope that's what comes across through my healing journey.

I grew up in church, attending three times a week, no questions asked. I accepted Jesus pretty early on as a kid. My childhood was what my husband likes to call "Leave it to Beaver," like the wholesome family TV show of the 1950's. My parents were straight-laced. No cussing, no drinking. I had a pretty sheltered upbringing. I thought everyone believed in God, and the majority of people had the same kind of life that I did. It wasn't until I was older that I began to see that things weren't always like that. I grew up very modestly. My parents didn't have a lot, but they made do and raised three kids. I, being the oldest of two brothers, was very bossy and princess-like. We never had any major life-altering things happen except when our house caught on fire when I was about 15 years old. My dad built the two-story frame house that we grew up in. It wasn't a total loss, but we had to live with my grandparents for 3 months while it was remodeled.

Over the years we had minor car accidents and illnesses, but nothing that shook me to my core. I lost my grandpa when I was 21. He had succumbed to his second battle with cancer. He was the only person I had lost that was close to me. As upsetting as it was to lose him, I had also watched his decline over the years and I knew he would be in heaven.

Still, nothing had prepared me for my own cancer diagnosis.

Preface

If you're reading this and you're a fighter or a survivor, thank you. The thing is, I didn't start out writing a book; I journaled for therapy. It was suggested to me at the very beginning of my journey, and surprisingly, it comforted me.

At first, I wanted to document the biggest thing that had ever come into my life, other than my children, of course. But it quickly became a tool that I would be able to use to measure God's love for me. I am a Christian first and foremost, but I don't categorize this book as a Christian or spiritual book. It is a real-life account of me. I am a real human being with countless flaws, and I want real human beings to read my story, whether they believe the same way I do or not. I don't want to edit out my reality for the sake of being a politically correct Christian. The God I serve loves me just as I am. I don't have to be perfect to be loved, accepted and forgiven and I want the world to know that they can have that same love too.

The first thing I was taught as a small child is 'God Is Love'. He's not some big scary ogre who's waiting to take you down when you're bad. He's the most loving, protective, perfect parent that has ever existed. I can only pretend to understand this kind of love. I love my two daughters more than anything on earth. I conceived them, bore them, and they are mine. But God created me. He invented human me. I can't imagine how much more powerful His love is for His own creation. So, in my journey through breast cancer, I not only found out a lot about myself, but I learned about God's true love for me and every human that has ever existed or ever will.

I invite you to walk in my shoes for the year plus that I wrote. This book is just a slice of my life, not all of it, so you will note that many of the entries skip over days and weeks. This is purposeful because this memoir is titled *You Don't Need Headlights to Shine*, and that is the part of my journey I wish to share with you. While *You Don't Need Headlights to Shine* reads like a journal, there will be sentences that seem unrelated and paragraphs that go off in many directions - but please know it is written exactly how it poured out of my heart into my notes app.

Yes, I wrote this entire book in my Notes app. :)

DAY 1

So my journey begins at the age of 43 and two weeks.

My very first ever mammogram.

I know I know. Three years late. But Covid, ok?

We lost two years of life already.

So in Covid years, I'm still 41.

But all that doesn't matter now.

Water under the bridge...

Well, my first mammogram, so I had nothing to compare it to. But it quickly became very memorable. I could tell immediately that things weren't "normal" and as I processed the things going on around me. It was like a movie. They were speaking to someone else. Then I'd realize they were waiting for me to answer. It wasn't a movie I was watching. It was my life.

I can go on and on about the things God has done for me in my life. My faith coming in clutch and always being firm. But the way he has orchestrated things lets me know I'm one of his favorites. And yes, I think God has favorites. He loves all of his children, but he does things for me that are extra. I just know it. So, at this moment, I want to document how solid my faith is. I can't see that it will waver, but what lies ahead is unknown. I'm sure I'll have moments (I'm told). But I know whose (favorite) child I am.

The mammogram appointment lasted all day. At the end, the radiologist came in to talk with me about the biopsy procedures that he recommended. At this point, I knew things were grim, but no one had technically said anything. He looked me in the eyes and said, "I want you to wrap your head around what I am saying right now before I do the biopsy, do you understand what I am saying?" Wow, I'll never forget those words. The sonographer was still in the room, rubbing my back. She said, "I had cancer too." "Too"? That means 'also'. She's saying I have cancer. She had cancer, I have cancer, I was still crying. She is still rubbing my back. She said the Lord got her through it, I needed to hear that. The Lord got her through because he will get me through too (also). Don't forget that. No matter how bad it gets. Don't forget He will get me through.

God put staff in place to push me through all the necessary screenings that I would need, which led me to find out I had breast cancer that very day. I know I haven't had a biopsy yet. But doctors know what they know. And it was obvious from the scans. The woman who did my sonogram was a Christian and a breast cancer survivor. She encouraged me. I believe God put her there for me. So, among my increasing worry earlier in my appointment, I had a thought that one of my girlfriends may be working in the building where I was being tested. She was in another facility a few doors down. I kept her updated on the testing that I had done. The Radiologist said they'd be calling me later to schedule two biopsies. One on each breast. They called and couldn't get me in for two weeks. I began to fervently pray for them to have an earlier opening. I asked a few specific people to pray that as well. The following day, my girlfriend, who worked at the other facility, called to tell me she had an opening for the screening that would do the breast that was least concerning. I struggled as I declined the offer. But that breast wasn't my worry. She said they were double-booked. She had pleaded all day for them to work me in for both biopsies, but they were adamant that it was impossible with their schedule. Meanwhile, my warriors continued to pray. About an hour later my friend called me back with 55 minutes left before closing time. They had an unexplained opening the following morning where they could do BOTH biopsies!! What? God, that was fast! So, pending my insurance approval and RX from my doctor, I accepted the appointment. Later I found out what hoops my friend jumped through to get that all done. They didn't even do the one procedure on Wednesdays at all. But for me, they did. And they were wonderful. But still without an official pathology result I could see the sadness in their eyes as they each looked at the scans. The way they treat you with extra sugar on top. A look of pity. The atmosphere in each room I entered had a cloud of heaviness. But I like things light and fluffy. So, I would talk and be my crazy self. Because I can't stand to be so serious.

So, my doctor was wearing a University of Florida Gators shirt. God, now you're being funny. My husband is a diehard Florida State Seminole fan. So, naturally, I had to joke with him because on Black Friday, The Seminoles had just beaten The Gators for the first time in 3 years. We joked and laughed and overall had a good visit, even though I am face down on a table with my boob hanging through a hole in the table and the table in the air while the doc is below me torturing my boob. But lidocaine is amazing, also from God.

They put a rush on my pathology, and hopefully, I would know something in two more days. Meanwhile, I have two other girlfriends who work at one of the top-rated cancer hospitals in the country called Moffitt. I was told by my radiologist that it wouldn't be premature for me to go ahead and reach out to them. They wanted to see me the next day! But I don't have the pathology report yet. So that's where I stand waiting for results to see what type of cancer I am up against. I'm hoping that in writing this, I can look back and see that my faith has only grown. And that Jesus has shown up in a big way more and more.

Day 4

Today was challenging, not for me but for my clients. I told several of them about what I was facing. I did not cry. My own composure astounds me. I feel like I'm telling someone else's story.

Some clients were very in control of their emotions. And most were not able to hold back. I hate making them sad. But they deserve to know what's going on. They have all shared their deepest secrets with me over the years. I've shed many tears with them all. This time, it just happens to be about me. They all say the right things when it comes to their future appointments. But we all know if this drags out, it will get old fast. I try not to worry about losing them, but I'm not losing some job that I can get somewhere else. I built this. God provided every one of these clients to me. So, on one hand, I know nothing can mess with that. But my flesh worries what would be left if this goes on too long.

I forgot to mention yesterday about God speaking to me through my favorite app. I was sitting on the patio waiting for the girls to get home so we could tell them I have cancer, *so naturally, I was on TikTok.* I follow all kinds of pages. Christian devotionals and conservative news sources. But mostly funny stuff. So, I get a good mixture of things. But yesterday, I opened TikTok, and 12 videos in a row were people starting out saying, "I have a word from the Lord" or "The Lord is telling me someone needs to hear this." Each video was a direct word from Him. I claimed every word out loud. As I scrolled, I could not believe what He was telling me. He knows how much I love to laugh, and when I need a good laugh, I turn to TikTok. But instead, my heavenly father spoke words that I could hear and claim as my own. Words of healing. And promises of the impossible being possible. It was so incredible. Nobody could ever tell me that wasn't Him.

Chad and I discussed how we would tell the girls and how we thought they'd react. We decided that it would be best if I could keep from crying, which I was able to do. I hate to cry—almost as much as I hate to puke. I've never liked those girly, sappy crybaby movies. I don't ever need "a good cry" like some women do. I like action movies and crime movies.

So, we told them. And in true kid fashion they did not react like any of the scenarios we came up with! They teared up and got quiet. Not the sobbing we expected. Eventually they went to their rooms. Shock I'm sure, processing. And today they seem good. I'm sure as we get further along things will change. But I told them we will try to keep life as normal as possible and that's my honest prayer.

Day 5

I'm awake early. I have a knot in my stomach. I'm sure it's nerves. I'm so nauseated. Chad is awake, too. He's holding my hands, rubbing my back. Today is when I hope the pathology report comes back.

I don't want to wait until Monday. I'm not a patient person at all. Chad always refers to me as Irene because his grandmother sure wasn't patient. It's not like having the pathology will lessen my anxiety, but I just need this ball to keep rolling. Chad has been really great and strong. I don't like people falling apart on me. He held me as I screamed on day 1. And encouraged me that we can do this and we'll get through whatever it is. He's called my friends and has even done the dishes! He walked the dog that he would never walk because that's not his dog. It's really been another miracle. I joke that if God's plan is to heal me, I won't let him know, so he'll keep being Mr. Mom.

As I was coming back from taking my daughter to school, I started praying out loud, "God, please let pathology call right now. I need to know. I need to know. I need to know." And I felt Him say, "You don't need to know. I already know. I am in control of this. I have gone before you." So I guess that's it. I have to be patient.

So, while I'm waiting here, being patient and patiently waiting and waiting for patience, I realized that I did not mention that the girls went to youth group after we told them my diagnosis. Before they were born, I prayed for their future friendships and relationships. And to see the people in their lives that I prayed for is such a blessing. Once their friends heard the news, they quickly took them to the altar and prayed over them. The girls' friends and their parents were among the ones praying. I have no way of knowing the future of their friendships, but it is so comforting to know they have support.

It's 3:30 pm on day 5 and I feel like I've been pretty patient. I keep checking my patient portal like a crack addict. Nothing. I don't understand how people can go through this. I feel like I've lived 30 years in the last 5 days. Do normal people have more patience than this? Like how long are people just ok with waiting? I'm consumed with this "thing." It's like a shadow following me around; I can't shake it. What did I used to think about? What were my normal thoughts? I can't even remember. I stare at my phone, wishing it to ring. The audacity of the spam calls I get!!! Don't they know people are waiting for important calls? I literally got a call from U.S. Customs and Border Security. Fool, call Joe Biden.

Day 6

For months now, I have been waking up between 2 and 4 a.m. wide awake. In the spiritual world, this is called the fourth watch. When Jesus was in the garden with His disciples and asked them to pray with Him, they kept falling asleep. They were supposed to be praying and keeping watch. Jesus was praying to the Father and asking Him to let this cup pass from Him.

I've learned that God likes to move and do things when it's quiet. So, when I'm awake during these hours I keep watch. Originally, I knew I was to pray for our country and our culture. The state of the world we now live in, and I knew there were other watchmen awake and praying at the same time I was.

So, looking back, I know God's been preparing me for something for some time. I wake up at these crazy hours, I pray and I go back to sleep. And I love to sleep. It's literally my favorite hobby. I'll pass up food for a good nap. So, when this first started happening, I was not happy. But I'm learning that this 4th watch is really the best time to connect with God. He prompts my spirit to pray just like he did with the disciples. And even though I want to sleep, I keep watch.

Back on biopsy day, before I left, my friend said she had someone she wanted me to talk with about her cancer diagnosis. One of her coworkers had gone through a double mastectomy and the whole nine yards. So we went into a small private room, and she and my friend came in. She began to tell me her story. We laughed and cried and exchanged numbers so we could keep in touch. She said her only regret was not journaling her experience. So, in essence, she's the reason for my writing. As we began to leave, my friend asked me if I realized who I was talking to. I said no, I'd never met her. The woman was one of my associate Pastors' wife!! We had prayed for her back in 2014 during her journey, but we'd never met personally. And here she was, encouraging me on my journey! Tell me God didn't put her there! It's just too much to wrap my head around.

Day 7

*"For He chose us in Him before the creation of the world to
be holy and blameless in His sight. In love."*
Ephesians 1:4

I'm looking forward to tomorrow *and also* full of anxiety. My friends and I have our annual favorite things Christmas brunch, where we each buy our favorite item of the year and give it to everyone in the group. We've done it for years now and it's so much fun. Meanwhile, I'm hoping to get a phone call from my doctor with the official pathology results. It's so weird to look forward to tomorrow when there could be so much dreadful news.

The feelings I have are so hard to explain. Of course, I know without a single doubt that I could receive a call that says there's absolutely nothing detected in my scans. That's my prayer, first and foremost, but I'm a realist, too. And a planner. And I want answers so I can plan. Gosh, I'm so sick of thinking about myself!! I welcome any distraction, except for my kids being jerks. But my thoughts are so consuming, it's exhausting. I long for the day that I can go an hour without it being in the forefront of my mind. It's only been seven days; I can do this. This morning in church, one of the passages the Pastor preached on was Ephesians 1:4.

So I cannot worry or be afraid. He knew my problems and loved me before He even created the earth. I told you I was His favorite.

Day 8

"But seek first His kingdom and His righteousness,
and all these things will be given to you as well"
Matthew 6:33

Every year, my friends and I have our "Favorite Things" Christmas brunch. Today was that day. I can't remember if I already documented this, which explains a lot, considering I have so much on my mind. We wear festive clothes, buy over-priced gifts, eat bougie food and have a blast. Then we go back to my house because I'm the designated Christmas cheer person, Dina is the Halloween queen, and we open our gifts. I messed it all up this year. Our reservations were for 10:45am and I had a video chat with my doctor at 10:45am. But I was not missing out on our party. So, I sat in the car (my friend Michelle stayed with me) while the others went in to be seated and had my video chat with Doc. She confirmed invasive ductal carcinoma in my right breast. She was sad to tell me. Tearing up. I still had no reaction because clearly, this was someone else she was talking about. My nerves were almost calm. One of my friends, who shall remain unnamed, brought me something to calm my nerves. Thank God it was beginning to kick in. So, I was able to ask the necessary questions. Meanwhile, I informed my two miracle workers at Moffitt, and they said to come straight over. So our brunch was rushed, all a blur. I honestly was out of my body floating around now that I look back. I wanted so badly to just be normal for two hours. My friends were amazing and raced me straight to Moffitt. Chad was able to meet me there with my films, and that's where it all became real. The saying is true that "it's all about who you know." I had the 10:45am video chat confirming my diagnosis, and by 1:00pm, I was in with the oncologist. It's absolutely unreal how God can just make things happen. I mean, He's God. He can do anything, but He literally just moves stuff around, and there are people out there who think it's just a coincidence. So, my girlfriend Beth, who works at Moffitt is there with me and Chad and the oncologist. They explain everything so clearly and kindly. All of my options available include pills for 5-10 years, radiation, surgery (lumpectomy, mastectomy) and the least chemo. Of course, I have already made the executive decision to chop these evil backstabbing boobs completely off. But I listen intently to every option. I need an MRI to make sure it's not in my lymph nodes. That will be another deciding factor. And Moffitt does EVERYTHING there. So, we went down the hall with Beth to schedule my MRI. Beth asked the scheduler to find me a good spot. She looked up from her computer and said with surprise

"Someone just canceled Wednesday." ARE U KIDDING?? Why do I get so blown away when God does this stuff? I mean, I pray, and He delivers even better.

So, like when you order French fries, you don't have to worry about the ketchup. It's gonna come with your order; just order the fries. So, I seek the father first, and He gives me ketchup. Heinz. Because the other brands suck! They're tomato water. See? I'm His favorite.

Also, He has given me INCREDIBLE friends. I'm positive that no one else has the kinds of friends that I do. And the prayer warriors!! I have so many connections with people and they each have their special gifts that they share with me. One day, I'll write a book about them all. The food, the kind words, the prayers, the devotionals that I receive from people saying the Lord gave them a word, and they thought to share it with ME!! That's a word straight from Him! Crazy, but why am I surprised? We should never be surprised when our Father delivers. As a mother, there is not one thing I wouldn't do for my girls. And the way He feels about me is that much greater. I'm not designed to fathom. I've gone crazy, Mama Bear, a few times in my life (not in a Christian way at all), and I know that intensity is there when evil attacks God's child. I know God is mad that I am facing this. But it's not from Him. But He will use this for His glory and I'll come out smelling like roses (unless that's not His favorite flower).

Day 9

"Praise be to the God of Shadrach, Meshach and Abednego,
who has sent his angel and rescued his servants!"
Daniel 3:28

Wow, only 9 days. If I could commit 9 days to exercise, we might have a future stripper on our hands. I think God filled me with the love of food to keep me chubby because I'm crazy enough that I would probably dance on a bar top somewhere. One of my more reserved clients suggested I name my journal Tata Tales, but Tatas seem like a more refined, classy name, and my titties are not classy; they're trashy. They betrayed me, so they are "titties" and belong in the trash. My new rack, however, will be referred to as TaTas because they will be upstanding citizens but without nipples. I'm still trying to grasp that aspect. I mean, I don't know for sure. I will meet with the surgeon on Thursday, but I'm pretty sure I won't have nipples. I wonder what the difference would be, let's say, between the fatty part of the back of my arm and my new boobs? Let's think about that as a woman for a second. Boobs are just a sack of fatty tissue. I am blessed (or cursed), whichever way you want to look at it, with lots of fatty tissue on my body, so from a husband's perspective, why haven't the back of my arms been as appealing all these years? Because of the nipple, right? But look, I'm not considering keeping these titties because of the nipple situation, and Chad and I have discussed all of this. He's adamant that it's my decision. I didn't need his permission anyway, but I respect it. So that'll be weird.

I do think that a mastectomy without reconstruction would really bother me. I've seen women that have not done reconstruction and I really do not think mentally I could handle that. I'm not a person who ever shows cleavage or really cares about that. I mean, I've spent $5000 on Invisalign for my teeth because everyone sees my teeth; no one sees my boobs. But... apparently, now a lot of people will see my boobs. I thought about selling tickets. "Farewell Titty Tour." I'm going to need something to supplement my income. Honestly, the reconstruction and surgery are the second scariest part of this. Chemo being number one, but we don't know if I'm facing chemo yet. Surgery is definite, and I don't like that kind of stuff. I would never choose to have a boob job just because of the surgery and the drains and the leaking and all that stuff. I don't want to see that, and I don't want to have it voluntarily. So, this is something I did not choose, but I will face it with all my dignity because Jesus will rescue me. My mom reminded me of the story in the bible of the 3 boys (Shadrach, Meshach, and Abednego)who were thrown into the fire because they would not bow to King Nebuchadnezzar. They said, *"If we are thrown into the blazing furnace, the God we serve is able to deliver us from it, and he will deliver us from Your Majesty's hand" Daniel 3:17*

So, I know my God will rescue me. But even if He didn't, I still trust Him. He still reigns and is still perfect, and I wouldn't change a thing.

Christmas will be here soon as well, and I have so much to do. Part of me just wants to ignore it all. Not Christmas. But all the shopping and nonsense. My brain can't handle all the "things." I'm rambling today.

Let's think about the power of the spoken word. I am absolutely terrible about saying out loud, "Ugh, I don't wanna work." Now, I love my job for the most part. I love hanging out with my clients, who I also consider my friends. I don't like "having" to work. I want to do hair only when I want to. But jobs don't work that way. Most days, I feel like I'm just socializing while making money. So, it's really not bad, and I shouldn't complain. I believe that the spiritual world, which is always battling all around us, can hear what we say. Angels and demons are constantly playing tug of war for us, using our words and actions either for or against us. So, when I say things like I don't want to work, I believe evil spirits hear that and use that to their advantage. I'm facing the possibility of not being able to work for a while. That's not what I meant when I complained out loud. But I think that even the demons know they can't have victory over me. I am covered by the love of Jesus. So, when my cancer was discovered, I was devastated and scared; that's the only victory evil can claim because Jesus will have the final say now and in the end. So that's why I have no tears to cry and no worry to give. Evil won't get another victory out of this whole mess. My Father is the risen King, and he overrides any spoken word, sickness, or challenge. And.... I'm his favorite.

Day 10

I'm high. My GP called in something for my nerves. I only took half, but I'm high. I'm so sleepy, too, and I have clients about to show up. My nerves are definitely calm, though. I guess that's good. So next time, I'll take 1/4 of a pill. In the morning, my anxiety is the highest. I still wake up early and feel jittery. My client is here, so let's see how this goes....

So, I made it through. My first client wanted to reschedule because he could tell something was off. I told him. We laughed. I said, "Boy, sit down. I can do this with my eyes closed. Reschedule? You've got to be kidding me. When? Because I have no idea when this crap will be over."

I just checked in for my MRI appointment. Everyone here at Moffitt is amazing. They must screen their employees to make sure they have a particular personality because every single person I've interacted with is delightful. Like I'm in an alternate universe where everyone radiates kindness and compassion. Even comedy! When you think about what kind of news is shared here, you would assume it would be dismal. But it's far from it. The receptionist for the MRI said I reminded her of an actress! I said, "Oh, I hope she's glamorous!' But what if I didn't have hair? It's hard to think of that as a possibility. I've pushed that thought away until just this moment. Being a hairdresser, I know how important hair is. Or how important we make it. It's really not the end of the world, our hair. Many people finally realized they'd live without their regular appointments during Covid. But we're slowly forgetting about that time. I love hair, obviously, and I was blessed with great hair as well! But sometimes, the day in and day out really grinds my nerves. It pays my bills and pays them well. But it's just hair. It's not even a living appendage. But we give it so much value. God knows my heart; I don't have to tell him how devastating it would be to lose my hair, not to mention the sickness. I watched my mother-in-law suffer through it all. At times, I was certain she might not make it. She was so strong, but I know she didn't want to be. Everyone tells you, "Oh, you're so strong," or " You can do this." I don't feel strong at all. But what are my choices? I've always said if this were to happen, I'd go straight to Moffitt and get a double mastectomy. But what if I never discovered these boobs were backstabbers? I mean, they've been part of my body since middle school, and I thought we were on the same team, so I figured we'd be together forever. But now I want to purge them from my life completely. How long would I have if we never even messed with it? I shouldn't say these things. But they're my thoughts, and that's what this is about. Documenting my thoughts so I can come back and see that this was a blip in time and how insignificant my ramblings are.

Day 11

*"So do not fear, for I am with you; do not be dismayed, for
I am your God. I will strengthen you and help you; I will
uphold you with my righteous right hand."*
Isaiah 41:10

I got home last night at 8:30pm from my MRI. I was so tired that I had a pity party on the way home. I went back and forth between emotions. On the one hand, I was amazed at the technological advancements we live with now. On the other hand, I criticized how far we still have to go. I laid on my stomach, boobs hanging down through a hole secured in, while a metal rod went between my boobs on my breastbone. Another rod across my ribs. Talk about being uncomfortable! I was sore already in the first few minutes of getting set up. The team of women working with me were so precious. Making sure I was comfortable (as you can get) and warm and my music was on (90s hits). They were great. But as I lay there in an encased coffin-like tube, my mind began to panic. I really had to convince myself to stay calm. It's so loud! Even with the headphones. That's the second improvement they could make: a silent MRI machine. The sounds are enough to drive anyone nuts. I kept my eyes shut the whole time, and laying on my stomach helped it not seem like a coffin but a massage table, without a massage and a metal rod up my chest. All the machines we have nowadays to detect cancer and other things are really incredible. To lay there or stand there and get a picture of our insides a few minutes later is astonishing. The brains that some people are born with are unbelievable. So, I went back and forth between cursing the machine, loving the machine, hating my body and loving technology. And, of course, asking God to calm me because He is there with me. On the outside, I seemed relaxed. But on the inside, I was acting a fool! By this time, I've lost track of how many tickets I could have sold to the titty show, but I'm definitely in the dozens by now.

That's another unsettling thing. Your boobs are just an object, a task at hand. Of course, I'm mad at them and don't care that they're being exploited. But they're still attached to me. And it's just weird. I know there are so many, much worse, diseases and problems out there in the world. But this is about my little world. And I will write about all the little discomforts of my journey in hopes that I can help anyone who may have to deal with backstabbing boobs.

When I got home, I was still a bit emotional. My mother-in-law had sent me a note through Chad. She had a hip replacement the same day I was diagnosed, and we haven't seen her yet. I opened the note. There was a smooth little stone that said "courage" in gold. The note said a little old lady gave her the stone to carry during her journey, and now she wants me to carry it. I really lost it. It was so special to me. Because I don't have courage. I'm just doing what I have no other choice to do. So Chad came home from taking the kids to church to find me a mess. He started the shower for me and said I'd feel better after a shower. He was right. He also cooked Alfredo pasta, and that was good too.

Today started out rough. I had an 8:30 am appointment with the plastic surgeon. I-4 traffic at that time is awful. We left in plenty of time, but of course, it still wasn't enough. I hate being late. fifteen minutes early is late. So, when the navigation kept saying 8:22, 8:35, and 8:52 arrival time, I was at full-blown level "10" anxiety. I texted Tina, my nurse friend. She said not to worry; 8:30 am was my check-in time. 9am was my appointment, just to arrive safely. So, by the grace of God, we made it by 9am. My plastic surgeon couldn't have been a more perfect fit for me! He was everything I like in a doctor. He was the appropriate age for a doctor, unlike my two previous radiologists who made Doogie Howser look ancient. Two young students came in with my plastic surgeon. Poor things. Seeing what their future body may look like probably makes them race to the gym as soon as they finish work every day. Anyway, my plastic surgeon explained all of my options. Chad was sitting quietly in the corner. The Doctor handed me an implant to look at. I tossed it to Chad. He got very awkward. I love it. We talked about taking tissue from the areas where I'm blessed with extra to make breast tissue. That's more invasive and longer recovery. More scarring as well. So, we decided on a double mastectomy with immediate reconstruction. The size of the cavity left by my oncologist will determine the size of the implant. I can always tweak it later. I will forever have breast augmentation covered under my cancer policy so I can adjust over the years. But I don't care about them being perfect, obviously. I've lived the last sixteen years with them deflated and hanging to my waist. So, a little ripple here or there won't bother me. I'm more concerned with healing properly. Then comes the nipples! He said they could make some! I don't even want to know how they do that. I think I'd just do tattoos. But that's much later.

So, I sent my mom and a few friends pictures of the new members of the Rader family. We all had a good laugh. Mom asked if I had named them yet. Nope. She came up with Tweedle D and Tweedle Double D. I like it! So that's it for now. I'm still waiting for pathology to determine if I need further treatment.

After meeting the surgeon, my nurse friends Beth and Tina suggested we meet with the chaplain. They said we would love her. And we did! It was comforting to talk with her and she prayed for us. She tried desperately to get Chad to open up. He was awkward again. I love it. We all know he has a softer side. It's just so deep down in there. He won't admit much, but I know this has been a hurdle. I wonder how different this would be for us if my reaction were different. If you had told me beforehand I would have had such a positive reaction I would call you a liar. But it's so true; you never know how you're going to be until it's there in front of you. So, at this point, I have at least 1.1 million people who are rooting for me and will do anything for me. So, I'm gonna sit here and see what I can conjure up for people to do, my own Make a Wish Foundation.

Day 12

*"In him we were also chosen, having been predestined
according to the plan of him who works out everything in
conformity with the purpose of his will, in order that we,
who were the first to put our hope in Christ, might be for
the praise of his glory."*
Ephesians 1:11

Today is not a good day mentally. I'm very down. Dr. Hoover called with my MRI results. The mass I have is bigger than they thought and it has two minions attached that were hiding under it. The original mass is 3mm. The two minions add up to 7mm total for all three. My lymph nodes are clear - praise God. And she assured me that my planned surgery could go on as scheduled. The kicker is I may need radiation after, and they're still not ruling out chemo. Radiation after surgery can compromise the implant. But it's still better to do the reconstruction as we planned. If there's damage from radiation, we can do damage control afterward. Since I chose to have the double mastectomy, it worked out well because, with this news, a lumpectomy would no longer be an option. Stage Two is the official diagnosis. So, I'm just not feeling cheerful, and I am mad that I feel down. I don't like it. I'm not crying or anything, just blah. Surgery is scheduled for January 3rd. This means I could potentially miss half of Presley's sporting events for the season, and that infuriates me. I wanted so badly for this not to affect my kids. I've never had to miss any of their activities.

Cancer really does suck! Nevermind, I'm good now. I took Presley to her doctor's appointment and the receptionist swore I was Presley's sister! She had a fit over my skin. She called out "Mom" from the desk, and I looked up and said, "Yes?" She said, "Oh my God, you really are her mom!?!" Made my day!! She asked to get a closer look at my skin and asked what my secret was. I said, "Girl, just wait until I get my new rack in a few weeks!" If she only knew what I had just been stressing about! My freaking chin hairs!!! I have to be in the hospital for two days. Do you have any idea how fast they grow? I'll go into the hospital looking like Presley's sister and come out looking like her grandfather!! It's so not fair. I have to reschedule my laser hair removal appointment, and who knows when I'll be able to go again? And I have to be on hormone blockers for at least the next decade, so who knows where else I'll be growing hairs. It's just too much right now. I knew something like this would happen. I've always joked with my girlfriends that if I were to be in a coma, they better come de-hair my face. Ugh, now the time is upon us. So the true test of friendship begins. And it's a bunch of bull crap that I won't care about what I look like! No one sees me without makeup ever! I gave birth with a full face of makeup and my hair done, and I kept the thermostat so low that my mom and my mother-in-law had to bundle up in the delivery room. I'm not sweating. That's another thing to add to the list of things I hate: puking, crying, sweating. I will care what I look like. Because when I'm better, I'll know everyone saw me look like hell, and I'll be mad.

Day 13

"And my God will meet all your needs according to the
riches of his glory in Christ Jesus"
Philippians 4:19

Today, I woke up early with stewardship in my heart. I'm fortunate that my parents were very obedient when it came to stewardship so it was a natural progression for me as a working adult. Stewardship refers to the tithe mainly, but it also includes anything that God gives us, which is everything we have. When we became parents, we dedicated our girls back to the Lord in a ceremony at church. I remember telling God that they were His and I was just in charge of them here on earth. It was very emotional to truly give them to God and know that no matter what happens, they are really His. I haven't done the best job of leading them the way I thought I would. I knew my faith was rock solid, so I didn't worry about building their foundation. But my faith doesn't get handed down to them. They have to build it on their own. So I'm ashamed that I haven't been a better steward in that. Pastor says when we are obedient to Him that we can receive God's blessing in many forms. When we tithe, you can't expect God to make you rich. Your blessing may come in the form of good health, skilled athleticism, or possessions. But being God's favorite is my favor from the Lord. I'd rather have none of the things I'm blessed with than lose His favor. Because I have received special treatment all of my life. I never knew it wasn't the same for everyone.

I have no idea why He favors me. I think maybe if He made me rich, I'd be a stingy old miser. Or if He made me skinny, I'd be a stripper. Not sure. I have never missed paying a bill. I have never gone naked (maybe topless soon). I have never gone hungry. And I even get most of my wants, too! I hope it doesn't come off as bragging. But I haven't done anything to deserve what I have been blessed with. I just try to be obedient to the things God lays on my heart. My very best friend from eight years old, Kathie, has very different views than I do. She's what I call a puritan. She's my soul sister. We are Yin and Yang. Her heart is very sensitive and she isn't able to watch crime shows or scary movies. She doesn't listen to modern-day country music (old Dolly Parton and Randy Travis are fine), where they talk about drinking and otherworldly things. They really affect her spirit. I, on the other hand, don't have that sensitivity to music or movies at all! I love all kinds of music. I've learned that we all have different levels of convictions with our faith and our morals because God made us all so unique. I believe that personal conviction is defined as a specific boundary of behavior that God has set for each person individually.

I used to feel like something was wrong when I didn't have the same conviction as others. But I know "I am fearfully and wonderfully made" (Psalm 139:14). That's what makes us all different, but also made in His image. The bottom line is I have tried my best to be obedient to the convictions of my heart and I have received His favor because of it. I could never do enough to deserve His love and abundant blessings. Just like my kids. Even when they're being complete brats, I still would do anything for them. I give them all their wants just because I love them. Because they certainly don't deserve them all the time. I always think that's how God loves me. So much more than I am even able to comprehend.

Day 14

"When you pass through the waters, I will be with you;
and when you pass through the rivers, they will not sweep
over you. When you walk through the fire, you will not be
burned; the flames will not set you ablaze."
Isaiah 43:2

In the words of one of my favorite 90s rappers, Ice Cube, "Today was a good day."

This diagnosis has given me a spirit of preparation. Like when you're pregnant, and you begin "nesting." You are driven to get things done and in order because once the baby comes, you have no idea when you'll be normal again. I like things a certain way in my house, and I don't like other people cleaning up. If we have company, I like people to enjoy their visit, and I clean when they're gone. So, all of this will be an adjustment. Chad and the girls have no idea how I like things done, but I'm ok with letting them figure it out. I know during recovery I won't care. But I don't want to come out of it surrounded by a zoo either. I know there are far greater things to concern myself with like my chin hair growing out of control, but I pride myself in taking care of the house and keeping it running smoothly.

God has given me a sense of peace that doesn't even make sense. I know I haven't faced the deepest waters yet. But I know who is asleep on the boat during the storm, and when it's time for Him to rescue me, He will. Faith is believing in the outcome before the problem has taken hold. At this point, I am so at peace that it's hard to believe why I am even writing this.

Day 17

He says, " Be still and know that I am God; I will be exalted
among the nations, I will be exalted in the earth."
Psalm 46:10

Today was the original date I was given for my biopsy. But homie (God) don't play that. In these seventeen days I've had so much progress it's hard to believe anyone could wait this long to have a plan. My first client today was a joy. She always is. But today, she really had something to talk about. She just recently had a kidney transplant. She was born with a genetic kidney disorder and has been on dialysis for years. She's only in her early 50s. She's always happy and never complains about having to get treatment; she still works full-time and keeps her grandson. As she told me her story of how God provided that kidney at the perfect time and how the doctors were in disbelief at how smoothly the surgery went, her eyes filled with happy tears. Her surgery was supposed to last several hours. It only took half the normal time and the kidney started working immediately with zero problems. She was so overcome with emotion and gratitude I couldn't help but join in. She thanked God for the life of the donor, and it melted my heart. Meanwhile, she hated to share her good news with me, considering my situation. I told her not to feel that way at all! My cancer has already been defeated. I just have to walk through the valley. She said we would both celebrate on the other side of all this, and I can't wait.

All through the day, I received messages from friends or clients checking in. I love it so much that I'm in the hearts of so many. One of my texts today said, "Just wanted you to know, you are on what I am calling my 4 am prayer list. Over the last several months, I have not slept as well as I used to. It has become very common for me to wake up at 4 AM. I have decided to use that time to pray for my friends. I just wanted you to know that I am consistently praying for you. "WHAT is even going on right now?"

On Day Six, did I not talk about this already? Let me go check. Yes. Yes, I did. This person had NO IDEA that I did this, so I sent her my journal entry for that day. We were both absolutely blessed by whatever God is doing. So, what is He doing? It's not just about me. He's working on so many people all the time, but this feels bigger than normal. Maybe because it's involving me this time? But I don't think so.

#Godsfave

Day 18

"Not only so, but we also glory in our sufferings because we know that suffering produces perseverance; perseverance, character; and character, hope. And hope does not put us to shame because God's love has been poured out into our hearts through the Holy Spirit, who has been given to us."
Romans 5:3-5

All these days have passed, and I've never said, "Why me?" I genuinely have not said that, wondered that, or spoken that. Now, earlier, when I spilled an entire tub of cat food on the floor, I said, "Why me?" among other choice words. It's crazy. The mundane things of life get me so ruffled. Stepping in a puddle with my new shoes, my kids texting me nonstop to check them out of school, me worrying about Chad wiping my butt, I should start taking a stool softener now. Why do bidets cost so much? Why are nipples such a big deal? All these can send me over the edge.

What I have asked is, "Why the inexplicable peace?" "Why am I not fearful?" "Are my feelings normal?" "Am I handling this the right way?" Sometimes, I'm afraid that I may be in denial, but I'm sure I'm not. I completely understand the entire saga. I fully grasp the diagnosis, which is not by any means a death sentence. I fully grasp the magnitude of the surgery, the healing process and the possible treatments that no one will rule out. Chad and I talked about how it feels like we've been dealing with this for months! It really consumes you. But why? Does it have to?

When people hear the news, why are they so distraught? Why was I so distraught the first few days? If you really break it down, it does suck, but I'm not dying. I'm going to get through this. So is it just sad because I have to go through it? Is that why we carry on about it? These are things I wonder since I've had so much time to analyze the situation. I love to analyze people and their problems. It's the best part of my job. I've had time to process and really look at the big picture. I know this is always something that will be part of my story, but in reality, it's just a "part." So many have reached out to say they've battled and beaten. And I would've never known. That'll be me someday. I'm not trying to belittle anyone who goes through this at all. I'm looking at it from my perspective. This is my diary, after all. It doesn't diminish anyone else's diagnosis, either. I wouldn't wish this on my enemy. As I've had time to reflect, though, my feelings about this whole thing have calmed down. I wonder if that's normal. You just get used to it, I guess, but I know that on surgery day, I could be singing a different tune.

My friend Paige and I always talk about deep stuff. I asked her about my faith faltering when the valley gets too deep. It's so easy now to trust God when I'm seemingly normal, and life is going on as usual. But what about the deep waters? Will I still really trust Him? I know He'll show up for me really big then. It's just unimaginable to have the peace I have now and expect it to be even greater. This has only highlighted to me how blessed I truly am. When I receive tearful hugs and condolences, I feel so bad for the person. Because I'm really ok with it, all my blessings now stand out like they're under spotlights. The blessings are so huge that, to me, it makes the cancer seem so small and insignificant. I truly hope I can come back to this entry and claim that I was right; Cancer is so insignificant compared to how big my God is.

I will not be shortchanged. I'm waiting to see what God will do next.

Day 19

"When the Lord takes pleasure in anyone's way,
he causes their enemies to make peace with them."
Proverbs 16:7

Most days, I have nothing to write. At the end of the day, I sit down and ask the Lord to help me write something to inspire my future self. And I swear on everything that He just gives me the words. Now, I'm not saying I'm Harper Lee or anything remotely close. But these words aren't mine. This journal started out as my words nineteen days ago. Now it is ALL HIM. For His glory. So I can reread His goodness.

So, anyway, I've always been a person who expects others to treat me the same way I would treat them. Disappointment comes when we project our expectations on others. When someone disappoints us, it's because we feel they should have behaved the way we would have. But that's not how it works. You begin to understand that the one hurting you has different battles going on. Or maybe they haven't been taught how to be a good friend. Now I know for a fact I'm not always a good friend. The Bible says, *"A man of many companions may come to ruin, but there is a friend who sticks closer than a brother."* Proverbs 18:24

We cannot rely on others to always be there for us. But Jesus will always be there. Some of us are lucky enough to have found those friends through life who have been there and will always be. I have so many friends like this. But I have also had my share of hurt. I'm ashamed to say that I am not a fan of second chances. Once I feel I've been wronged by someone, it takes quite a while for me to get past it. After time, I will forgive them and move forward, but I try to never allow that to happen again. Sometimes, God allows friendships to fall apart to protect us. Maybe that friendship would've led you down the wrong path, or maybe you would've been hurt much worse. And God protected you from that. I eventually work through it to have peace with God and move on. The Bible says we are to make peace as best we can, and if the other person cannot agree, it is no longer on us. So, in many circumstances, that's what I've done. I'm at peace with God in many situations that I feel are out of my control.

In saying all of this, a miracle has happened today. A person from my past has been diagnosed with the same cancer I have. Her mastectomy is before mine. We have not spoken in over a decade and I didn't even have her phone number anymore and never thought I would ever need it. But God had other plans. He's a comedian. He likes to sit up there and laugh at the plans we make for ourselves. He says watch this! I'm not gloating when I report this, but God led me to reach out to her. When He told me to, I said you've got to be kidding me!?!

So I got her number and sent her a message. I told her I knew we didn't exactly part ways on the best terms, but I heard of her diagnosis, and I wouldn't wish it on anybody. I also told her I was praying for her complete healing. She immediately responded with the same sentiments, and she wanted us to stay in touch through our journey. I can't handle what is going on.

I literally can't get the lump (not cancer) out of my throat.

Day 20

"See if there is any offensive way in me, and lead me in the way everlasting."
Psalm 139:24

I watched this movie one time, 'The Shack.' I read the book as well. It's pretty brutal. The book/movie itself is amazing. It revolves around the unimaginable crime of an innocent child and the father's quest to find peace. He questions God and his faith like any normal person would. That movie revealed God to me in a way that I had never thought of before. God reveals Himself to us at the exact time, in the exact form, that we as individuals need. We are not made to fathom His love for us. He created every human ever born. He loves every one of us. Even the most despicable, evil, worthless piece of crap you can imagine. He loves them, too. He is incapable of not loving them. Pastor says there are three things impossible for God to do: He can't stop loving you, He can't do anything evil and He can't make you return His love. When bad things happen to us, it is not from God. People like to say, "Oh, God is testing you" or "God is punishing you," but I don't believe that's true. God can't perform something bad. He turns EVERYTHING bad for His good. To shine His goodness. He may allow for something to interfere in our lives to draw us closer to Him, but He can't create havoc. And, after all, we live in a sinful world. evil rules here. Bad things will happen to good people. That's just life (Thanks Adam and Eve). But in every bad situation, if you pay close enough attention, as a child of God you will see His presence in that situation. His love is irrevocable. With that being said, of course you have to accept Him to receive all these blessings. What the movie showed me was how deep God's love really is. It's the closest that I could ever come to understanding how He feels about me. There is nothing I can ever do to lose His love. The same way I feel about my children, except so much bigger. My brain can't handle it. So, when I look down at these stupid poisonous boobs, I know they aren't from God. But God will use these titties to shine His beacon of light. And I'm here for it! And soon I will have one of my good and perfect gifts after this trial, new TaTas! I just have to stay steadfast.

Day 21

When Jesus spoke again to the people, he said, " I am the light
of the world. whoever follows me will never walk in darkness,
but will have the light of life. "
John 8:12

I survived the ninth level of hell today. Some may call it purgatory. Most refer to it as a home improvement center, I like to call it Blowes. I despise that store. I'm a shopper at heart, addicted actually but that is the most boring shopping in the universe. I can find more excitement in a convenience store. I think it stems back to my childhood, where I partially grew up inside a lumber store. My dad built the house I grew up in, and we made countless visits there. The smell of lumber and dust and just pure boredom puts me over the edge. Unless we are shopping at Blowe's specifically for me, I don't want anything to do with it. Today was kind of for me. But not totally. Chad's been amazing about preparing for my level of comfort, so with the upcoming cooler weather, we like to utilize our patio even more. We picked out lighting and heaters and a handheld showerhead for my recovery. Easy right? Wrong! Most women I know know what they want. That's me. I can decide on a dime what I like and don't like. But men.... I don't know all men. But my man.... He over-analyzes everything. He always makes the best decisions for our family. He's very smart with money and taking care of our vehicles and our home. The years he shaves off his life expectancy from the stress of overanalyzing is unbelievable, though. Standing in the lighting aisle, hotter than absolute hell, pondering over the size of a bulb, LED vs regular, Edison or traditional. I. Don't. Care. But Chad doesn't understand the concept of I don't care. I am particular about many things. But when I'm not, I'm not. I just want to get out of that stifling store. Could you imagine him inside of a women's department store? Ain't fun. He's so bored and doesn't understand why I have to look in every department and touch everything. But how ironic is that when it comes to how he likes to shop at Blowe's? Every aisle, touching every adapter, cord, plug, remote, and battery. Puke. I long ago stopped inviting him to shop with me so I could go in peace. In Blowes, though, I'm not allowed to stray too far because I have to be close enough to hear him "think aloud." Lawd, have mercy. I'm using my C-card from here on out, so I never have to go back there again. (I was inaccurate earlier. Blowe's is more like the sixth or seventh level of hell. I reached level nine when we got home and I had to help Chad hang the lights).

This morning, Pastor preached on what Christ's birth means to us as Christians. I probably have it all mixed up, but what I remember is God IS love. He came to save the world, all of us. As His children, He not only wants us to succeed but to be significant with the purpose for which He created us.

Reconcile with others as best you can, even when you haven't been the one to do wrong. Because God forgave our sins, and He has never been wrong.

That was hard for me to hear. I hate to apologize anyway, but to realize that God forgave me when He is perfect really got me. I never thought of it that way before. We are to pray instead of panic and worship instead of worry. I'm so glad my default setting seems to be these options; I would have never thought so before now. But maybe I haven't hit the biggest bump yet. That worries me a little. Will I still learn to pray instead of panic?

Day 24

"You then, my son, be strong in the grace that is in Christ Jesus"
2 Timothy 2:1

I hate lizards. I went into my shop this morning and started to get ready for the day. As I was sweeping, a lizard jumped out. Tears ran down my legs. Ugh! Why do they even exist? I'm convinced if Adam and Eve had never sinned that those things wouldn't be here. Frogs too. They're so unpredictable. Most things, when they're scared of you, run away. These vile creatures will come at you. Stupid. I watch it to make sure I don't lose track of it while peeking outside and praying that my next client is here and that she will take care of it for me. No such luck. I stare at this thing with pee-pee in my pants. It could be half dead, but who trusts that? I say, 'God, I will fight this cancer with all I've got, but please don't make me catch this lizard!' I check outside one more time. No one to rescue me. So I pulled up my big girl panties (wet with pee) and wrangled that little devil out the door. It may or may not have been 100% alive, but it doesn't change my fear level.

I started to think about how fearful I am of frogs mainly and lizards. And I realized I have never had an actual fear of this cancer. Initially, when I got the news, I was shocked, sad, scared of the unknown. But never fearful of the actual diagnosis. I still have some unknown factors floating out there. But I have absolutely no fear. It's so insane to me. I don't say these things to boast. Truly. I am recording my actual true feelings. No fear. From the first minute, God was already covering me with grace and mercy. He has not only set my path, but He has gone before me. He never said our entire path would be smooth, but He guarantees His presence on our path. He never said we would not have troubles and trials but that when we did, He would carry us. So that's exactly why I feel like I'm describing someone else's life and circumstance right now, because He's carrying me. I'm not actually walking this path, just like the poem *Footprints in the Sand*.

Day 25

*"For the Spirit God gave us does not make us timid,
but gives us power, love and self-discipline."*
2 Timothy 1:7

Today has been the toughest so far. Seeing your child hurt is the absolute worst. I would do anything to take hurt from them. I wish I could give her the peace that God has given me, like just take it off and hand it to her. I know that's not possible because then we could just pass around God's goodness all the time and never feel hurt again. For me, I'm learning that feeling bad is an opportunity for me to grow. Not just spiritually, but self-growth. I wish I could pass that along to her as well. In my forties, I've learned so much about myself and about life. It's true what they say about not going back to your youth without taking our newfound wisdom with us. I like my older self better. Not my backstabbing boobs, of course. Or my giant butt. But the growth in my maturity. I still have quite a ways to go though. I still want to unleash on anyone who hurts my kid, and I will get nasty really quick. But that's only for my kid. For myself I've learned to calm down some. I've also learned how to communicate better, my real feelings. I'm still very blunt about my opinions, but I'm learning to present them a little differently. But, when it comes to my girls, I lose control. Today, I didn't exactly lose it, but I was definitely caught off guard and felt extremely overwhelmed with all the little things. I don't just feel it; I know it; evil is trying to bring my family down. Our Pastor always says you're not important enough for the devil himself to attack. He goes after the big fish. There's only one Lucifer. And he's not omnipresent like God. But his demons all work overtime. So yes, I feel like the forces of evil are attacking my family directly. The roller coaster of emotions today has been way too much. Each individual thing on its own is more than manageable, but all at once it just got to me.

I'm so thankful for learning scripture from my youth group days, which has brought me so much comfort now.

- "So do not fear, for I am with you; do not be dismayed, for I am your God. I will strengthen you and help you; I will uphold you with my righteous right hand" Isaiah 41:10

- "Praise be to the God and Father of our Lord Jesus Christ, the Father of compassion and the God of all comfort, who comforts us in all our troubles so that we can comfort those in any trouble with the comfort we ourselves receive from God." 2 Corinthians 1:3-4

- "Your word is a lamp for my feet, a light on my path." Psalm 119:105

Day 26

"Those who hope in the Lord will renew their strength.
They will soar on wings like eagles; they will run and not
grow weary, they will walk and not be faint."
Isaiah 40:31

This verse came to me several times today through TikTok, my Bible app, and a book that was gifted to me to help me through this journey. I'm not even sure what exactly I'm supposed to document about this verse, but it's obviously a word from the Lord. The whole chapter talks about how mighty our creator is and how nothing compares to His vastness. Mountains are minuscule in His hands. He knows each star and calls them my name, never forgetting a single one. He never tires or needs a break, but He will give us rest when we are weary.

It's so nice to be able to just shut off and shut down and wait on Him. I can just hand it all over and go to bed. When I wake up, I'll have renewed strength for the day. Sometimes, I have to do this several times during the day. Just hand over all the thoughts and unknowns and walk away from it. I don't have to carry it. Maybe this verse was just a reminder to wait on Him. I'm looking forward to tomorrow with renewed strength.

Day 27

*"Every good and perfect gift is from above, coming down
from the Father of the heavenly lights, who does not change
like shifting shadows."*
James 1:17

I have told the story of how I learned of my diagnosis hundreds of times. Between all of my friends, clients and family, I have the story memorized. But every time I tell it, I find myself using phrases like "out of body," "not really there," or "watching someone else's life." Today, I got confirmation of what those out-of-body feelings really were. It's what the peace that passes all understanding feels like. It's inexplicable. That's why I don't understand what I'm feeling. I have the true peace of God over me. And He has filled my heart with joy in spite of my diagnosis. So many have commented on my positive outlook, that even I am shocked about. Now, it all makes sense. I've never felt His true overwhelming peace because I've never walked through a storm of this size. I really am as ok as I seem on the outside. I really am at peace. And I really am highly favored. So, on the Eve of my savior's birth, I will carry His peace with me because that is why He came.

Day 28

"Take delight in the Lord, and he will give you the desires of your heart."
Psalm 37:4

Christmas Day is so different since my kids are older. It's still fun to see them happy, but the "magic" isn't there. They know all the gifts they're getting and there's no cookies and milk left out for Santa. I can't say I had a bad Christmas at all; just different. I delight myself in my kids' response to Christmas. I love seeing it through their eyes. That's part of the magic. So, when they lose that childlike reaction, it makes Christmas feel a little different.

This week, I learned about the above verse. I'd had it memorized since I was very young, but until now had never been truly taught its meaning. I thought it meant that since God is our Father, He wants to give us all of our desires. Just like I do with my girls, that is partly true. The beginning of the verse, 'Delight yourself in the Lord, ' means 'extreme pleasure or complete satisfaction.' Only when we are completely satisfied in Christ are the desires of our hearts in tune with His will for us. And our desires become His desires for us. When we think so desperately we want or need something, and we pray fervently for it but do not receive the answer we expect, we should make sure we are satisfied in Him first. Then, the desire of our hearts may change.

Since my diagnosis, I have a renewed sense of urgency to see what God has to say to me every day. It's become a desire for me. In the process, my heart's desires are changing right in front of me. Of course, I desire to be healed from cancer, but it's weird that this thing I hate has caused me to lean closer to Jesus. So, I can't really be mad about it. Now I hate these backstabbing boobs for sure. That'll never change. But I wouldn't be seeking Him right now if it weren't for the diagnosis. I was stagnant before. Sometimes, God allows something to cross our path that moves us. Otherwise, we'd have kept on going just like we were. So, in a sense, it sounds sick, but I'm thankful for this bump in my path(cancer). It has put a giant spotlight on my blessings and pushed me into the hands of Jesus.

Day 29

*"And God is able to bless you abundantly, so that in all
things at all times, having all that you need, you will
abound in every good work. As it is written: 'They have
freely scattered their gifts to the poor; their righteousness
endures forever.' Now he who supplies seed to the sower and
bread for food will also supply and increase your store of
seed and will enlarge the harvest of your righteousness. You
will be enriched in every way so that you can be generous
on every occasion, and through us your generosity will
result in thanksgiving to God."*
2 Corinthians 9:8-11

Today, Mel treated me to a mani/pedi before my surgery. Of
course, I didn't know she had planned to treat me. Mel has such a
quiet, calming spirit about her. She's been there for me in ways only
she knows. We spent the afternoon giggling and relaxing and topped
it off with our favorite root beer. Later that night, our family went out
to eat and came home to watch a movie.

I decided it was time to get ready for bed. As I'm in the shower,
an incredible wave of sadness washes over me. I didn't see it coming,
especially after the nice day I had. I can't stop the tears from coming,
and all kinds of worries go through my mind. I know God is not the
author of fear, worry or doubt, so I try my best to suck it up and remind myself of all the scripture I've memorized over the years.

I think about the old friend I reconnected with who is having
her mastectomy tomorrow. And the fear and uncertainty she must be
having at this moment too. So, I prayed for her. I can't imagine if she
was able to sleep peacefully knowing what lay ahead. I still have a full
week to go and I'm breaking down. I've always told my girls that sleep
will cure just about everything, so I took my own advice and went
to bed. Even with a sedative, I was still fitful all night. I really hope

this doesn't continue for the week. I've never wanted time to hurry up and stand still at the same time. Just get these boobs off so I can stop thinking about it all the time. But then I think about what a circus freak I might look like. Where did these thoughts come from? I don't care about that stuff! So sleep did, in fact, help, and I wrote this the morning after. God's promises are renewed each day. I look forward to seeing clients all day and not having any pity parties.

My prayer is for the Lord to give me so much peace that I can give it away.

Day 30

*Now faith is confidence in what we hope for and assurance
about what we do not see.*
Hebrews 11:1

An entire month. God has shown up every single day for an entire month. He's always been there, but what have I failed to see before now? Yesterday, my friend from my past had her double mastectomy. I messaged her the night before, and she responded, saying that she would let me know how it went. I had no expectation of hearing from her any time soon because of the intensity of her recovery. But when I woke this morning to a long message from her at 7am, my heart leapt. She is doing AMAZING! She's texting me like she is completely normal. Telling me every detail. I can't believe it! We hadn't spoken for years, and the morning after her mastectomy, she messaged me! It's too much for me to handle. God is using someone unexpected to bless me! It's incredible who God chooses to use and place in our path. This cancer, meant to bring me harm, has only brought me nearer to Him. I'm sure that's the exact opposite of what that evil intended.

He has placed countless people in my life for various reasons. He put my clientele together with specific people who have always been a blessing. I am in awe almost continuously. When my old friend texted me this morning, I wept at His goodness. I don't deserve to be blessed in this way. But He says I am worthy of His love, and His grace is sufficient for me. He knows the number of hairs on my head (I pray I get to keep each one), and I am more precious than rubies. He sent His son to be crucified for Me; this I know, for the Bible tells me so.

Day 31

"Many are the woes of the wicked, but the Lord's unfailing
love surrounds the one
who trusts in him"
Psalm 32:10

At my initial visit with Dr. Hoover, she discovered that my heart skipped a beat. She asked if I had ever been told that by any other doctor. Chad told her it only happens when he's around. So, today, I had to get an EKG before I could be cleared for surgery. It turns out my heart is perfect—it just has extra beats. So when Chad accuses me of being 'extra,' I really can't help it.

Surgery is quickly approaching, and I find myself thinking about everything I do as in BC (before cancer) and AC (after cancer). This is a time marker in my life, and I hope that it's not different from AC. But what if it is?

Today, we hung out with friends. I never thought about cancer. It was wonderful. The girls acted silly with their friends, which always cracks me up, and we went to lunch and had ice cream, too. It was so normal and I loved it. I pray that AC will go back to times like these with one exception: that I will never take 'normal' days for granted. That I will always see God's blessings the way I do now with these very eyes. Because I have always had a life so full but lacked the vision to see it.

Day 32

"Children's children are a crown to the aged, and parents are the pride of their children."
Proverbs 17:6

Three days until life-changing surgery. I still have the perfect peace of God. Otherwise, I'd be freaking out, right? I keep waiting for the freakout to come, but it doesn't. His peace really passes all understanding. I am living it right now. One of the Pastors I follow described it as the eye of a hurricane. I'm in the eye. There isn't chaos around me by any means (other than my kids). But there is a constant spiritual warfare all around me. I believe that what evil has sent to destroy me is being fought off by angels right at this very moment. I'm that important to my Father. He sends armies to fight for us. All we have to do is invite Him in. So, I can just sit here in complete peace while battles are being fought and won on my behalf.

When I was little, I had a specific memory of my mom's mom, my Mimi. She was very ill most of my life, but this day she was healthy. I went to her house, and we made peanut butter cookies and hot chocolate and swam in her community pool. But the one thing that stands out to me from that day is that she had a huge notepad beside her bed. Pages and pages of numbered items. I asked her what it was. She said it was her blessings. She told me we were to count them one by one. Until this very moment, I didn't know why that memory stood out to me so vividly. But now I do. I have listed things I'm thankful for verbally in prayer. But I am starting a list of my blessings. I could never have enough paper in all the world.

Number one on my list is my salvation. When I think back to the legacy of my family and how Christian morals and beliefs were taught to me, I have to go way back and thank God for my great-grandparents who made a stand for Jesus. Without them, my grandparents and parents may not have ever known Jesus and I may not have salvation right now.

Day 33

"Because of the Lord's great love we are not consumed, for his compassions never fail. They are new every morning; great is your faithfulness."
Lamentations 3:22-23

New Year's Eve. Most people are anxious to start a new year. I have many friends that 2022 was not good for them. A lot can happen in a year. I've always wondered why we put so much emphasis on a "new" year. Like the turn of a calendar can bring so much change. I'm not one for resolutions just because of the time of year. If I want to do something, I just do it. Starting out 2023 in the hospital with major surgery is not how I'd like to begin, but I'm positive that it'll only get better from there. This year, my faith will see the biggest growth in my 43 years.

Instead of waiting for the turn of the calendar, we can wake up every morning with God's mercies renewed. I'm thankful for that promise.

Day 34

"For Christ's love compels us, because we are convinced that
one died for all, and therefore all died. And he died for all,
that those who live should no longer live for themselves but
for him who died for them and was raised again."
2 Corinthians 5:14-15

My oncologist called me at 6pm today, New Year's Day, a Sunday, her day off. People like her don't get a day off. You can tell from speaking with her that she is never "off." The level of knowledge she has is unfathomable to me. You don't get to the very top of your field by taking days off. She wanted to let me know about a new procedure they are making available to me that helps prevent swelling in my arm from the removal of lymph nodes. Because I'm a hairstylist, this is a huge concern for me moving forward.

I am beyond thankful for her and Moffitt. The work they do there is in their blood. They never stop thinking, learning or caring. I trust them wholeheartedly because my God delivers. He has given me the very best from the beginning. Not just the beginning of this stage of my life, but always. I look back at things or situations and know that my loving Father placed things in my path at certain times so that I could have the best of the best. I have never done anything to deserve all these blessings and never could if I lived a million years. All I did was say yes to God's love and the rest is history.

#Godsfave

Day 35

*"Two are better than one, because they have a good return
for their labor: If either of them falls down, one can help
the other up. But pity anyone who falls and has no one to
help them up. Also, if two lie down together, they will keep
warm. But how can one keep warm alone? Though one
may be overpowered, two can defend themselves.
A cord of three strands is not quickly broken."*
Ecclesiastes 4:9-12

Surgery Eve. I have no words. The outpouring of love is incredible. I have people rallying behind me who only know me because I'm on their church prayer list. I've been added to countless lists and can literally feel the comfort and peace on me like a blanket. I've had visitors, gifts, phone calls and texts. It's beyond anything I could conjure up in my wildest dreams.

My friends are too many to count, my cup runs over. It's 10pm and my heart is full. His peace is sufficient, and my day was FILLED with friends, physically, emotionally and spiritually. God is my shepherd; I shall not want. I can sleep peacefully tonight, knowing I am completely covered in prayer. I don't even have to utter a word tonight. He knows my heart and those who are petitioning on my behalf. He loves me more than installing LED lights in my child's room at 10pm the night before these tits come off. I would do anything for that kid. But if she or Presley ever ask me to put up those God-forsaken LED lights ever again, I will not.

Good night, *You Don't Need Headlights to Shine*; I'll write again as soon as I'm able with my new cohorts Tweedle D and Tweedle Double D Part 2 (DD) coming soon.

Day 36

*"Trust in the Lord with all your heart and lean not on
your own understanding; in all your ways submit to him,
and he will make your paths straight. Do not be wise in
your own eyes; fear the Lord and shun evil. This will bring
health to your body and nourishment to your bones. Honor
the Lord with your wealth, with the firstfruits of all your
crops; then your barns will be filled to overflowing, and
your vats will brim over with new wine. My son, do not
despise the Lord's discipline, and do not resent his rebuke,
because the Lord disciplines those he loves, as a father the
son he delights in."*
Proverbs 3:5-12

Surgery day. I Slept like a champ. Let's do this. Bye-bye, backstabbers. Hello Double D's.

DAY 37

I feel like I'm on fire...
I took meds, but I am still so uncomfortable.
My armpits are burning and my sternum.
The drains are pesky too. Pulling against stitches.
I feel like I have heartburn in my entire upper half.
I have to record all of this so I never forget how God
has held me through this whole time.

*"A friend loves at all times,
and a brother is born for a time of adversity."
Proverbs 17:17*

Tweedle D's are in. This hurts immensely. More later.

It hurts like I imagined it would. I feel like I'm on fire. When I had gallbladder attacks, it felt like a burning sensation. This is that. It's so tight it feels like I would think an asthma attack would feel. Doc said my tatas will never sag! They better not with all this pain. I took meds, but I am still so uncomfortable. My armpits are burning and my sternum. The drains are pesky, too. Pulling against stitches. I feel like I have heartburn on my entire upper half. I have to record all of this so I never forget how God has held me through this whole time. He has never failed me and I continue to receive so many blessings. The girls brought me flowers. And some were delivered to the house with a card that said, " To the bravest woman I know." It wasn't signed. They were from Chad. He has been so great to me already. He even picked up our cat Olive with his own hands and took her out of my room. Opening up himself to a possible allergy attack. My Knight in Shining Armor.

I've been asleep for 6 hours—the longest stretch yet. It feels like an elephant is sitting on top of me. I'm not sure how people get through this voluntarily.

Day 38

"Therefore do not worry about tomorrow,
for tomorrow will worry about itself.
Each day has enough trouble of its own."
Matthew 6:34

Cancer sucks.

Thank you, Jesus, for your unfailing word. It never returns void. Thank you for holding me right now during my pain. Your grace is sufficient.

Now back to how cancer SUCKS! Considering all of this, it's not all that bad. I'm so thankful to have the cancer removed. How many people can say that 38 days after diagnosis, their cancer was taken away? I'm thinking not many. I've heard of people having to wait three months or more to have surgery, carrying their cancer while it continues to grow. I haven't had to. The pain is manageable, so I'm thankful for modern medicine and my husband, who is truly in the midst of "for better or worse." He's been my rock. I can't believe the things he's willing to do for me. I continue to be overwhelmed by the genuine love and concern pouring in for me. Who knew I was really that likable? I'm so opinionated, and you never know what I'm going to say, so I figured I'm not everyone's cup of tea. But I guess people like some crazy flavored tea because I have never felt so loved.

I'm trying not to cry; I have that stupid lump (not cancer) in my throat. I still have the joy of the Lord right now, and it's so insane to me. I wish I could bottle it up and give away the comfort and peace I have. I know friends right now who could use it so much, and it is overflowing in me. I don't know why God has chosen to favor me, so I've never done anything exceptional on His behalf. I am only His daughter, and I guess that's enough. So, for this day, I will concentrate on managing my pain one day at a time and not worry about later or tomorrow because God is already there and making my path smooth.

Day 39

"Therefore encourage one another and build each other up,
just as in fact you are doing."
Thessalonians 5:11

I saw my boobies. I was so scared to look. Not bad. Not bad at all, really. I was so worried I'd look like a freak. They did cat eye incisions around the nipple toward my armpit. It wasn't the incision I had thought initially, but it really does look very good. My plastic surgeon was the first doctor to do a face transplant in the United States. I'd say he could stitch a boob with his eyes closed. My boobs haven't sat this high since, well… never. I have four drains, two on each side. They're stitched into my skin. They have to be emptied 3-4 times a day, measured and recorded. Chad does it without a grumble. It's more than just emptying fluid; you have to strip the drain tube, too, to remove all the fluid without tugging on my stitches. He's pretty gentle, which isn't his typical MO. I constantly call him a caveman because of his aggressive movements.

The girls have been really good about keeping up the laundry and dishes and Chad vacuumed today. I need to fake a relapse so they won't think I can do this stuff anytime soon. My pain is very minimal, and I'm done with the narcotics; over-the-counter medicine is enough. A muscle relaxer every now and then to help with spasms. I have a special mastectomy pillow that helps me sleep comfortably, too. I wear a special top with pockets inside. I call it my uni-bomber top. The drains go inside the pockets and look like grenades. We've had so much food and visitors, and it helps the day go by. All in all, it was a good day, and my heart is full.

Day 40

"He will be the sure foundation for your times, a rich store of salvation and wisdom and knowledge; the fear of the Lord is the key to this treasure."
Isaiah 33:6

The Bible mentions 40 days several times. When God destroyed the earth with a flood, Noah and his family were in the ark for 40 days and nights. When God told Moses to climb Mt. Sinai and gave him the Ten Commandments, he was gone for 40 days and nights. When Jesus, during his ministry, went into the wilderness, He was tempted by evil every single day for 40 days and nights. He did not even eat—40 long agonizing days.

I can't imagine any one of those scenarios for myself. I've said many times that I've lived 30 years in the past 40 days. But I have not been tormented. I've had food and shelter, friends, comfort, and a timeline of what my situation would likely be. I didn't have to climb a mountain or fight the devil off of me. I didn't have to care for stinking animals in close quarters with no end in sight (even though I do scoop the kitty litter sometimes (barf).

40 days is a long time. But in all of these situations, including mine, one thing is certain. The Holy Spirit was very present. He never left Moses. He never left Noah. He never left Jesus and He for sure has never left me. It's hard to comprehend the stories of the Bible because we can never relate to ancient inconveniences, but to me, it had to be so much harder back then. The modern comforts we have makes it easier to trust God. We are so blessed with physical comforts. Back then, they didn't have anything, but they still trusted Him. Or maybe I have it backward; we are so comfortable that we think we don't need Him and forget that everything we have is from Him. Back then, they had no choice but to cling to Him. Either way, times get tough, and times get easier, but God is always steadfast.

Day 41

"Do not store up for yourselves treasures on earth, where moths and vermin destroy, and where thieves break in and steal. But store up for yourselves treasures in heaven, where moths and vermin do not destroy, and where thieves do not break in and steal. For where your treasure is, there your heart will be also."
Matthew 6:19-21

My friends have storehouses full in heaven for what they've done for me. They can't brag on themselves, but I can do it for them. My friends have nourished my soul through this process. And for them, it seems like it's no big deal. It's what friends do, right? But they will never know how much it has meant to me until they get to heaven. I had no idea how much I depended on interaction with others. Through my job, I socialize so much, even on days when I don't feel like it. But I know that's what keeps me going. I love visiting with others and hearing about their lives and normalities. Now that I'm unable to interact as I would normally, I am craving that intimacy I have with my clients and friends. Some days, I would be exhausted from all of the stimulation it can bring, but I know now that I really want it.

Chad has a pretty big treasure storage up there, too. He's had to do things for me that, at our age, we didn't think we'd have to do. We laugh every night about what an ordeal it is to put me to bed. I have a CPAP machine; I have 4 drains that have to be emptied. I have to strap on this huge mastectomy pillow, fluff a million pillows all around me, countless pills and finally, he can tuck me in. I look like some kind of alien. I really hope I don't have to return the favor any time soon. Once Medicare kicks in, I'll make sure we have a plan that includes a home nurse. I'm not built to handle these things. But God has blessed me abundantly, and I still don't know why, but He definitely favors me. I'll take His favor any day, any time. I'll go through this as far as He wants me to go because I know the plans He has for me are better than any dream I could dream. So, for my friends who have blessed me, keep it coming because your mansion in heaven is bigger than mine, and I'm coming to stay—a lot.

Day 42

"My command is this: Love each other as I have loved you.
Greater love has no one than this:
to lay down one's life for one's friends."
John 15:12-13

God continues to show up in huge ways. I stay in a constant state of amazement. He continues to provide in the most unlikely ways. Using unassuming people to bless me. All throughout the Bible God uses the most unassuming to do His work. David (a shepherd boy) against Goliath. Moses led the Israelites (with speech impediment) and lowly shepherds to spread the news of Jesus' birth. God can use anyone to do His work. People are literally coming out of the woodwork to bless me. It's true that you can never comprehend the plans He has for us. Through this process, I have opened myself up to be used however He decides. Because I don't want to miss out on anything else He has for me. And I want others to see that this cancer is nothing compared to my God. A friend sent me this quote yesterday:

ONE DAY, YOU WILL TELL THAT STORY ABOUT HOW YOU
OVERCAME THAT BATTLE YOU WENT THROUGH, AND
GOD WILL SEND YOU THE EXACT PEOPLE
WHO NEED TO HEAR THAT STORY!

I can't wait for that day, and I can't wait to tell it a million times.

Day 43

Today was blah. I'm not depressed. It's a combo of boredom, irritability and frustration. I tried to sleep a lot to pass the time. I haven't felt like reading either, which is unusual. I'm anxious to see the doctor soon. These drains are obnoxious, but I'm thankful to Jackson Pratt for inventing them. I think they really do help with the healing process. The whole thing has moved so fast and I feel stagnant. Ready for drains to come out and then whatever's next. One of my friends who had a mastectomy last year with chemo was messaging me. She hates the hormone suppressant she is taking. Likely the one I will be taking. She says she's depressed and cries all the time. I really don't want to take it if it's like that. I know I can have a different experience, but I have no way of knowing until I start it. That's bothering me too. I have moments of cry-laughing. I don't even know if I'm laughing or crying. It's so annoying. Chad doesn't know what to think, either. One of my drains is giving me a problem. So we got out the "What to Expect When You Cut Off Your Boobs" manual. We decided we should call the nurse. I got a little emotional out of nowhere. It's weird, I don't like it, and I want to get better. The nurse didn't think there was cause for alarm. I will see her in two days anyway.

Day 44

"Rejoice in the Lord always. I will say it again: Rejoice!
Let your gentleness be evident to all. The Lord is near. Do
not be anxious about anything, but in every situation,
by prayer and petition, with thanksgiving, present your
requests to God. And the peace of God, which transcends
all understanding, will guard your hearts and your minds
in Christ Jesus."
Philippians 4:4-7

Every day gets a little better. I have more movement without pain, more range of motion, and I am able to do a little more for myself. It's not anything crazy, but brushing my teeth without discomfort is huge, and washing my face with both hands is priceless—little victories.

I spent several hours with friends today, and that always does me good. But I sure am exhausted when they leave. I take a couple of naps a day. My naps are getting shorter, too. Tomorrow, I will see my plastic surgeon to hopefully get these drains out. Gifts and food continue to flow in. Presley's friend Ella went to NYC for New Year's. She knows how much I love ornaments. She brought me an NYC Liberty ornament. I love it! She wrote the sweetest card, too. The way God provides is beyond what I can ever predict. I have His favor for sure, and to see it happening is mind-blowing. Chad and I go back and forth between disbelief and "Of course that's God." No Big Deal, But I have prayed for God to provide any and all needs we may have. And He did. After the initial shock of it all wore off and God gave me peace, I have had zero worry about our bills or my healing or when I'll get back to work. It will all happen as my Father wants it to. And for the first time in my life, I don't even care about the timetable. Ain't even worried one bit.

Day 45

*"I waited patiently for the Lord ; he turned to me and
heard my cry. He lifted me out of the slimy pit, out of the
mud and mire; he set my feet on a rock and gave me a firm
place to stand. He put a new song in my mouth, a hymn
of praise to our God. Many will see and fear the Lord and
put their trust in him. Blessed is the one who trusts in the
Lord , who does not look to the proud, to those who turn
aside to false Gods."*
Psalm 40:1-4

On our way to the doctor! I'm so excited! Never thought at for-
ty-three I'd be excited to see the doctor. I pray I can get these drains
out. I think I would feel almost normal again. Except for these jugs! I
asked Doc in the hospital what size he thought they were, "A bit more
than a British handful," he said. Whatever that means. Do Brits have
big hands? Small? I don't know. But the Tweedle D's sit up so high I
feel like I have heartburn all the time. My backstabbers never sat this
high. I'm sure everything will settle in time. But I'm most excited not
to wear a bra! Maybe never again! No nipples=No headlights.

I just left the Doc; three-quarters of the drains are out! Hallelu-
jah!! It felt so good! I go back next week and maybe this last little devil
can come out so I can have a real shower.

The drains really did help so much. They keep the swelling down
to almost none. So now that they are out, I'm having swelling and
tightness that I didn't have before. It's just uncomfortable. It feels like
when your milk comes in after the baby is born. Taut skin stretched
and hard. I still wouldn't call it pain. Just annoying. My body will
start absorbing the fluid, which wasn't much anyway except for the
remaining drain. It feels so heavy. I'm sure I'll get used to the feeling
of something foreign in my body. I've been asking my fellow implant
friends how they feel and what to expect.

Day 46

*"Praise be to the Lord , for he has heard my cry for mercy.
The Lord is my strength and my shield; my heart trusts in
him, and he helps me. My heart leaps for joy,
and with my song I praise him."*
Psalm 28:6-7

Ten days ago, I had what is referred to as "major surgery." I sit here in awe of what God has brought me through. I know my journey is not over, but so far, it has been nothing like I expected.

Waking up from surgery, there was pain, immense pain, and nausea. My first memory was the nurse asking if I felt sick. Tears were streaming down my face because I couldn't speak. The pain was so bad. Without my contact lenses, I could not see; I was disoriented. The voices around me assured me they were doing everything they could to help with the pain. As they wheeled my bed toward my room, they told me Chad and my parents were there, but between my tears and the pain, I could not see them. They grabbed my hands and told me I would be ok before I was quickly settled into my room. I don't remember much after that until the meds kicked in. Even now, I can't even explain the pain, only that it was intense.

Our plan was for Chad to go home and get the girls so they could see me, and then my parents would take them back home. But Chad didn't think they should see me the way I was. I wanted to see my girls so badly. I promised him that once he got back to the hospital with them, I would be much better. And I was! I remember them all giggling a lot, but when I asked what was funny, they never had anything to say. Apparently, I was high. Which had to be better than what I was. I was even able to eat Mac and cheese for dinner. I had a good visit with the girls before my parents took them home.

Then Chad and I proceeded to get ready for a night in the hospital, which we hadn't done since the girls were born. I was a little worried for Chad. He has nightmares or night terrors, especially when he's tired. Mainly when he's had a traumatic event at work or he's worked several shifts without sleep. So naturally, even in my medicated state, it crossed my mind that this traumatic day could lead to an event. Luckily, we never got more than maybe an hour or two of sleep at a time before someone was coming in to check my drains, take my temperature or peel back the sheets to look at Tweedle D and Tweedle DD.

He wasn't able to get into a deep enough sleep to have any terrors. He can't help it. He gets it from his mother. One of my favorite pastimes when we get together with his family is when they tell sleepwalking stories. There are so many and they're hysterical. I've been arrested in the middle of the night; he's gripped my wrists so tightly there should've been marks; there have been snakes in our bed, lizards, spiders. If he happens to see a snake on TV before we go to bed, it'll be in our bed later that night. But he did good!

To say it hasn't been traumatic for me is true. I've already forgotten the pain, and the soreness is not at all what I expected. In my mind, I know my diagnosis, surgery and journey ahead are huge things. When my mother-in-law went through it, it was terrible. We worried so much about her, but she was so strong. So, I know this is technically a big deal. But God has shielded me from it all. I've had moments of sadness or self-pity, but not what I thought I would. I am definitely being carried through this and I don't plan on God putting me down any time soon. But that's the thing, I can't plan on anything. God may let me get to a point in all of this and take a step back. I mean, He's God; He can do whatever He wants. That's ok, too. Whatever the plan is, I'm all in. He's proven His love for me over and over and He does not fail. If I look back on this day and I've seen the worst of it, I will see He still has not failed me. So right now, 10 days after a double mastectomy, I am really doing just fine.

Day 47

"Vindicate me, Lord , for I have led a blameless life; I have trusted in the Lord and have not faltered. Test me, Lord, and try me, examine my heart and my mind; for I have always been mindful of your unfailing love and have lived in reliance on your faithfulness. I do not sit with the deceitful, nor do I associate with hypocrites. I abhor the assembly of evildoers and refuse to sit with the wicked. I wash my hands in innocence, and go about your altar, Lord , proclaiming aloud your praise and telling of all your wonderful deeds. Lord , I love the house where you live, the place where your glory dwells. Do not take away my soul along with sinners, my life with those who are bloodthirsty. I lead a blameless life; deliver me and be merciful to me. My feet stand on level ground; in the great congregation I will praise the Lord."
Psalm 26:1-9, 11-12

Today, I woke up with a heart full of gratitude. I figured it was a good time to write thank you cards. I have dozens of people to thank and I don't want to forget anyone. I hope every single person knows what it meant to me that they gave of themselves. Tears streamed down my face as I wrote card after card. I have so much to be thankful for.

The Bible says, "And the King shall answer and say unto them, Verily I say unto you, Inasmuch as ye have done it unto one of the least of these my brethren, ye have done it unto me." Matthew 25:40 So even when we do the smallest action for others, we have done it for the Lord. God gets a blessing through others as they are blessing me. My list is very long and continues to grow each day.

I ventured out of the house today. The coldest day of the year so far. I bundled up as best as I could with this one pesky drain left.

Presley is in Ocala for the long weekend at a tournament, and it kills me that I'm not there. So, it was just Chad, Harper and me. Harper and I like to go antiquing, so Chad dropped us off at one of our little spots and he went to Blowes. Afterward, we had lunch. It was so nice to be out for a while. I did really well; I did not overdo it, and walking is very good for me, especially at this point. Not a single person in the store knew of my circumstances. No one could tell I had a double mastectomy 11 days ago. I thought about what the other shoppers could be hiding on a seemingly normal shopping day. Maybe they have a diagnosis far worse than mine or buried someone they love 11 days ago. It could be anything. Everyone goes through stuff. I didn't want any of those people to see or know what I was going through, but I am thankful that Jesus knows. I don't have to tell Him anything, I don't have to pretend, and I don't even have to explain. He knows my heart even when I can't muster a prayer. That is so comforting.

Day 48

"If you believe, you will receive whatever you ask for in prayer."
Matthew 21:22

Pastor has been preaching on fearless prayer, big prayers that move God. I'm guilty of 'comfort' prayers. Asking the Lord to provide, protect and heal—mundane daily utterances. And there have been times in my life when I've prayed deeply and boldly. There have been days that I didn't pray at all. Prayer is HUGE. It is direct communication with my creator. The Bible says to pray without ceasing, that means constant dialogue with Him. Forty-eight days of fearless, deep, bold prayer will change you. It hasn't changed my situation; it has changed me. I am so thankful that God is using my cancer as a chance for me to grow closer to Him. I could have responded so differently to all of this. I am so glad I didn't. I am shocked to discover this about myself. But in that discovery, I have proof of Jesus. The next time someone asks me how I know Jesus is real, I will tell them this. I have been asked about my faith many times. I have stories of God showing up in situations. But this story, being told I have cancer and reacting with a truly grateful heart, is insanity. That can only mean the presence of God. I think God is insane in the way He works in my logical brain and in the way He uses disease, divorce or tragedy for His good. He is not insane, but my human mind cannot make sense of it.

I'm not able to fathom how God will use this cancer for His glory. I'm not created to 'get it' and that's ok because my faith will carry me into the unclear path ahead. And I'm excited for the first time to see where He will take me. And I hate surprises. I mean hate. I'm a planner. I like to have things prepared. I start packing my suitcase weeks before a trip because I want to make sure I'm prepared for every possible scenario. But for this next 'trip,' I cannot prepare for the destination, and I'm ok with it. Because I trust the *"Event Coordinator"* with my whole life.

Day 49

"For I know the plans I have for you," declares the Lord,
"Plans to prosper you and not to harm you, plans to give
you hope and a future."
Jeremiah 29:11

In our house, we make jokes out of everything. Even my cancer isn't off-limits. Within days of my diagnosis, I was pulling the "C card." I've said before I like to keep things light and fluffy, never too serious. It came naturally, "Hey, Presley! Come empty the dishwasher! I have cancer!"

"Harper, clean the litter box; I have cancer!" "Chad, take me to my favorite restaurant; I have cancer." But now, I don't have cancer anymore. God has healed me. Yes, it was removed from my body, but He put every step into place to make that happen, and quickly. Praise God, the backstabbers are gone! So, while it was fun to have an excuse to get out of things for a while, I can't really use my "C card" anymore. And even though we joke a lot, we never speak of the chemo treatment. That is the 'Voldemort' of our home, 'he who cannot be named' like the evil villain in the Harry Potter movies. We don't joke about that. We never discuss it; it's just off-limits somehow. I can't say I've worried about it because I truly haven't. But it has a small space in my subconscious. I've come too far to start questioning God's plan for me now. A week from today, I'll know more about what to expect.

Cancer didn't come from God, but He is using it to grow my faith. If chemo gets a starring role in my life, then He will use that as well. I'm also very aware of the power of the spoken word. I've been studying how the forces of evil will use your weaknesses against you. I started a few years ago practicing the power of the spoken word when it came to sickness. If I felt like my throat was scratchy, I didn't dare say it aloud. Then COVID-19 came. I continued on but added major vitamins and kept taking magnesium for my painful hip.

Magnesium fights inflammation, which is what COVID-19 loves to attack. I didn't get sick. I was exposed many times. Chad had it at least half a dozen times. I never spoke of it. I used to say things like, 'Oh, I think I'm getting sick,' or ' I don't feel good,' or 'I think I'm getting something.' I completely stopped saying any of it. I noticed that I wasn't getting sick even when those closest to me were. But then I get cancer, so go figure. I have no idea if the spoken word was really that powerful or if I've just been on a lucky streak of avoiding the crud, but I'm not going to change it. It's risky enough for me to write about it, but this is a document of my journey. So I will continue to not speak of 'he who shall not be named' and continue to pray and continue to ask my friends to pray that 'it' will not be part of my journey. And as long as they allow it, I'll keep pulling out my C card here and there whenever it suits me; of course, you know, I say this with humor. It is one way I work through all of this!

Day 52

"Each of you should use whatever gift you have received
to serve others, as faithful stewards of God's grace in its
various forms. If anyone speaks, they should do so as one
who speaks the very words of God. If anyone serves, they
should do so with the strength God provides, so that in all
things God may be praised through Jesus Christ. To him be
the glory and the power for ever and ever. Amen."
Peter 4:10-11

On our way to Moffitt, hoping to get my last appendage removed. I'm a little worried that he won't do it. I will be super disappointed if he thinks I need it another week.

But...drains are out!!!! I am done with that! It felt like having extra arms that were completely useless but required constant, gentle attention.

My doctors are so knowledgeable, confident and kind. It takes a very special person to be a nurse as well. The things they see, smell or touch don't seem to faze them. They showed so much gentleness and compassion toward me and never acted like they had any other patient to deal with. They really are angels and even though they probably think they're just doing their job, it's more than that. Their patients are dealing with life-altering situations, and their sensitivity to it helps immensely. My doctors and nurses are truly the extended hand of God. He gave them a gift and they are using it the way He intended.

Day 53

I showered like a normal human being last night! You just never realize the mundane tasks of daily life are really luxuries. I wash my hair every day. I have very oily skin and hair. So, it has not been easy for me to skip several days without shampoo. If I skip one day, my hair literally looks like you fried bacon on it. Yesterday I went to the doctor with two-day hair. I really thought it would be ok. I used dry shampoo and styled it. I was so paranoid about it. I kept asking Chad if it looked greasy. He said it was fine and I was being crazy. By the time I left the doctor's office, my hair looked like I had stood in the rain. Disgusting. But at least I was able to clean my body really well. Chad and I had a great system for getting me clean. We dubbed it the elephant car wash. It was such an ordeal to wrap up my drains and wash all around without letting water drip anywhere near my incisions or drains. We rigged up all kinds of trash bags with hair clips. I would giggle almost the whole time because we must've looked like a circus act. But we don't have to do that anymore! And I hope never again! I threw away all of our rigged-up stuff and all the stuff that we used to clean my drains. So refreshing! I put on clothes like normal, no more wincing from stitches or a pulled drain. I got to sleep on my side without a mastectomy pillow. I wore normal pajamas without special pockets to hold my drains; just 17 days of discomfort felt like months. I'm so thankful it was only 17 days.

Day 54

*"My salvation and my honor depend on God ; he is my
mighty rock, my refuge."*
Psalm 62:7

Until last night, my incisions were covered by eight inches of surgical tape. My plastic surgeon offered to remove it at my last visit, but
I wasn't ready to see the scars. It's no wonder, with the amount of soap
I was using in the shower, that I looked down to see half of one side
detached. As I began to remove the rest, I panicked. I don't wear my
contacts in the shower, so I don't see very clearly, but as the old, dried
blood washed away, I worried that maybe my incisions weren't healed
all the way. For some reason, the tape made them feel secure. And I
did not want to see what was under it. My skin looked pruned from
the tape and wrinkly. I got really upset. I grabbed my phone that was
playing best of the 90's, and texted Chad to come. As soon as he saw
why I was upset, he told me how good it looked. How amazed he was
at the healing process so far. He told me not to worry that every day,
they'd get better and better. I still didn't want to look. He helped me
take the other side off.

Those eight-inch pieces of tape had given me so much comfort.
Now they were gone. I wasn't ready to see what I looked like. I'm still
not ready. It's not like my boobs before looked great. I had to scoop
them up from my waistline to put them into my bra. But they were
what I was used to. I'm not ready to get used to seeing something else
yet. I know all the comfort God has given me through scripture is for
moments like this. Part of me feels so silly for getting upset. I get to
live because of these scars. I get to throw away all of my bras because
of these scars.

Once I finished my shower and we got my PJs on with all the other nightly routines, I ordered scar cream and vitamin E oil. It arrived
this morning. So, as I sit here writing this entry, I have applied scar

cream to 16 inches of life-saving scars in hopes that they'll be minimized. My next step in making them look normal will be in a minimum of three months. I will get 3D nipple tattoos. Of course, my nipples won't be 8 inches wide, but they should help disguise part of it. My plastic surgeon is an excellent plastic surgeon. All of my stitches are internal, so I know the scars will be the best possible outcome. I'm just not ready to look. I didn't realize how much comfort the tape gave me. I feel like it held them together. Even though I know they're healed, it makes them seem more vulnerable now.

Enough gloom and doom. I haven't had any visitors in a while, and today, I'm expecting several. So, today will be so uplifting for me. I hope I can make it all the way through without getting too tired. I'll definitely need a nap this afternoon to prepare myself.

I had such a good time laughing and doing something normal that I completely forgot about Tweedle D and Tweedle DD. It was fantastic! Every once in a while, I'd move a certain way, and I would feel an uncomfortable tug that brought me back to reality. My friends really make me forget for a while, and I crave that feeling. I did so well that I think we should try to go back to church tomorrow. Even though it's really late, I'm not drained like I have been, so as long as I sleep well tonight, I don't see why we shouldn't go in the morning.

Day 55

*"Salvation is found in no one else, for there is no other
name under heaven given to mankind,
by which we must be saved."*
Acts 4:12

We made it to church this morning and lunch afterward. Between that and my friends visiting last night, that was about it for me; I needed a nap for sure. My armpits feel bruised and sore. I get asked about my pain level quite a bit. I have no pain, just mild discomfort like post-workout soreness. I haven't worked out in many, many, many years, but I've never forgotten the feeling of how it hurt to sit on the toilet after a leg workout or how it would hurt to use the blow dryer after an arm workout. The muscles that are sore from surgery aren't ones I've exercised before so it's a weird feeling for my armpits to feel bruised. I've had sore pectorals before, so that's about the same. I still can't bring myself to look at the incisions. I've been applying scar cream and it feels so weird. It's numb, but I can feel it. I get queasy when I touch it. It gives me the absolute creeps. I hate it. The skin feels lumpy, and I rush to put the cream on so I can wash my hands. I keep thinking I should just look and get it over with, but then I'm stuck with the reality of it and can't go back. I'll try another day. Tomorrow, I have a big appointment. I have no feelings about it, not good or bad, just nothing. Peace, I guess. As of last Thursday, my labs weren't back yet. So, unless they come in Friday or early tomorrow, I may not have anything to discuss at my post-op.

This morning, Pastor continued his sermon series on being fearless in our faith. God wants us to speak boldly about what He's done for us. When Peter and John were thrown into prison for healing a cripple in Jesus' name, they didn't back down. They boldly claimed that their power came from the Messiah.

I have not been bold about what Jesus has done for me. I share this journal with other like-minded friends, and some have been encouraged by what God is doing. That's not bold.

I ask too many questions. I question myself. I don't question God's ability to reach someone. I second-guess myself. I worry that a non-believer wouldn't understand my story, or they would think it's strange. Or worse, they would read it and feel nothing at all. I know that God only asks for the faith the size of a mustard seed, but I feel like half of a seed. I'm not bold. I've known this for a while, and I've avoided writing about it. This is a HUGE thing I'm working on. I battle with being bold because of my weakness. I would tell someone else to be bold in their faith without blinking an eye. But I can't tell myself. I know this is all the devil getting into my thoughts and trying to discourage me, and he has. I know all the things, I am worthy, and God will work on others; all I have to do is obey. It's very simple, yet it's very difficult to actually do.

I'm being very raw in my struggle right now, and I may choose to keep this entry private. But, at the same time, I need to be encouraged to share my story boldly.

DAY 56

I haven't been in denial, I knew it was possible.
But I haven't allowed myself to dwell on the possibility.
As the doctor explained, I began to face reality.
I was barely holding it together.
I needed to pay attention to what she was saying.
I got up and got some tissues and calmed myself down
while she continued to explain.
It's not the end of the world, she said.
And it's not...

*"No weapon forged against you will prevail, and you will
refute every tongue that accuses you. This is the heritage of
the servants of the Lord , and this is their vindication from
me," declares the Lord.*
Isaiah 54:17

DoomsDay. And it was.

Not the worst, but not the best. I was not prepared to hear "positive lymph node." It came as a complete shock. I haven't been in denial. I knew it was possible. But I haven't allowed myself to dwell on the possibility. As the doctor explained, I began to face reality. I was barely holding it together. I needed to pay attention to what she was saying. I got up, grabbed some tissues and calmed myself down while she continued to explain. It's not the end of the world, she said. And it's not. There could be far worse news, I know that. The original plan was to have the special lymph node surgery if a node came up positive, but since then, my team has met and decided that radiation without the lymph surgery may be the better option. If I do the surgery and then have radiation, I could most definitely develop lymphedema.

So, right now, the plan is to skip that procedure. My oncologist will have a special meeting on Thursday to see what all the other doctors think about my case. Meanwhile, I'm scheduled with the radiologist on February 7th.

My surgeon is sending me to the chemo doctor. She just so happened to be able to see me tomorrow. Normally, she wouldn't be able to get me in for quite a while. I think that means chemo is back on the table.

So that's where I am. Thank you, Jesus. I don't have to wait months to find out more—just 24 hours.

I'm numb, just like these boobs. I can't feel anything. If I let myself feel, I'm afraid of what that would look like. I don't want to get upset for nothing. But the doctor said I needed to prepare myself. And once again, there seemed to be a cloud hanging over the room.

God has undoubtedly prepared me for what I've already faced and, apparently, for what is to come. I will go back and read about all the blessings He has given me so that when I leave the doctor tomorrow, I will have armed myself against any weapon formed against me.

Day 57

"But now, this is what the Lord says— he who created you, Jacob, he who formed you, Israel: 'Do not fear, for I have redeemed you; I have summoned you by name; you are mine. When you pass through the waters, I will be with you; and when you pass through the rivers, they will not sweep over you. When you walk through the fire, you will not be burned; the flames will not set you ablaze. For I am the Lord your God, the Holy One of Israel, your Savior; I give Egypt for your ransom, Cush and Seba in your stead. Since you are precious and honored in my sight, and because I love you, I will give people in exchange for you, nations in exchange for your life.'"
Isaiah 43:1-4

Driving now to meet the chemo doctor. Yesterday, Dr. Hoover could not say whether or not the chemo doctor would recommend treatment. But she told me to prepare myself for that being most probable. Due to my young age we want to use every precaution. The chances of recurrence could be 10-15 years. Or maybe never. But if I choose not to follow recommendations, recurrence before the end of my life expectancy is most likely. I want to live a life of no regrets. Knowing I fought as hard as I possibly could. Knowing I used every resource available to me. It could still come back at any time, regardless of how I fight. But my conscience has to be clear, knowing I've done it all to stay with my family for as long as I can. Dr. Hoover has fought the battle herself. She lives a life with no regrets. The patient before me had cancer years ago and declined further treatment, and now it's returned. I think she will always wonder if she did the right thing. I don't want to live that way. So, whatever the chemo doctor recommends today, that is what I will trust, knowing my Father has already gone ahead of me and prepared the way.

Just met with my medical oncologist (chemo doctor). She recommended, with the size of my tumors, stage two, and my age, that chemo would, in fact, help. The goal is to cure me once and for all so that I may never have to go through this again. Chemo will be once every three weeks for four treatments total. I do not need a port. It will be an infusion through my vein. My hair will fall out. Some people don't get sick, but if I do, it will be a few days after the infusion and last for a few days. Once that is complete, I will have radiation, and I will meet with the radiologist in February to see how many of those I will need.

There are options to have a wig made from my own hair and donor hair. The price starts at $1600. I had really considered this, but how comfortable would it be? It would make me hot and itchy. But I'd feel obligated to wear it if I spent that amount of money on it. I really don't want to work without hair, and I guess I'll be working through this, which right now seems so inconceivable. I have no idea how I will manage all of this. I want to see my clients more than anything. I just can't work out in my mind how that looks. I know I still have time before I go back, and I know God already has it planned, and it will be better than anything I can invent on my own. So I'll have to shelve this worry onto the stack I've already given Him. The valley is low like they said it would be. And my redeemer is here as He promised. I just want to get home and scream to the top of my lungs. I want this to not be part of my story. I don't want chemo to have a starring role in my life. I'm mad. I'm sad. I'm worried about all the things. My job, my kids, my bald head!! What if I have a jacked-up head? My mother-in-law had a beautiful round head.

When it's all said and done, I know I can look back at how it all worked together for my good, because I do love Him. #hesmyfavetoo

Day 58

*"The Lord himself goes before you and will be with you; he
will never leave you nor forsake you. Do not be afraid; do
not be discouraged."*
Deuteronomy 31:8

It's still January and I probably won't be done with all of this until
June. 58 days has already felt like years. I just got off the phone to
schedule my first infusion for next Tuesday. I could have waited another week, but what would be the point? I'm glad things have moved
smoothly and quickly. Appointments seem to 'appear' right when I
need one. So I'm going to roll with it. Avoiding the inevitable for
another week would make the anticipation worse. It's like ripping off
a band-aid. If I don't give myself too much time to dwell on it, I don't
have time to get upset. Today probably could've been my lowest day,
except I had a constant flow of visitors. From the moment I got up, I
was busy until the first visitor came by, so even though subconscious-
ly, I had a lot going on, it was not at the forefront of my mind. When
a visitor is here, I can answer questions without emotion because it's
just a story to tell. But if I was alone all day, I know I would've been
a mess. Even now, I don't have the lump in my throat; it's as if this
is someone else I'm talking about. The scheduler I spoke with went
ahead and made my 2nd infusion appointment as well. She asked me
all kinds of things about my future appointments when I had no clue
what I was really doing yet. I'm sure all of it will make sense after next
week.

We told the girls about my treatment last night. I was so busy
trying to hold myself together that I didn't notice their emotion.
Chad finished explaining things to them, and the night seemed fairly
normal. Today, I got a text from Harper that she meant to send to
her friend. It expressed her concern for me and that she didn't know
what to do. It absolutely broke my heart. I know they are being af-

fected by this, and that infuriates me. I can handle this, but them? Why should they even need to be exposed to this kind of worry? I remember shaving my mother-in-law's head after her first treatment. The whole family was there in her kitchen. I set up a makeshift salon and got to work. She was so unaffected by it, seemingly. I remember laughing and joking. But for all I know, she could've bawled her eyes out after we left. Maybe I'm just not there yet in my journey. But if I had to shave my head today, I would not be able to handle it. Yesterday, I tried to wrap my mind around that certainty. Not ready. I know hair is just hair. I know it'll grow back. But it's the in-between. I will most likely be bald by next weekend. And it won't even begin to come back until maybe April/May? After that, it only grows half an inch per month, so by Christmas, I might have 4 inches of hair. Ugh. If I keep my eyebrows and lashes, that will be HUGE to me. At least I could wear makeup and look halfway normal. When people lose their lashes, I think that's when they look 'sick'. But the plus side is that maybe I'll lose my chin hair once and for all!! All of that laser hair removal paid for nothing! Who cares as long as it's gone? I don't have time to worry about all this crap and plucking too. Something's gotta give.

I was invited to a luncheon with my neighbor and am really looking forward to it. I'm not sure when I'll get to dress up and go out for a while. Even though I don't plan on being sick, I still have to be careful not to catch anything. My immune system will be weak. They'll give me something to help, but I'll need to be careful all the same. Then, on Friday, I begin a full day of scans, and Chad will definitely be checking out the cafeteria. I start at 6:30am and finish around 11:30am, then start another series of scans at noon.

No one can plan for the bumps or mountains that come up in life. This interruption was nowhere near my radar. But as I am learning to surrender fully to God's plan for me, I can cross this mountain and know for sure that whatever is waiting for me on the other side will be more than worth it. So I will pull up my granny panties, and suck it up, and get to the other side of this mountain so I can see what God has in store for me. I told Him that if I have to go through this, it must be for a really good reason that I can't see or know right now.

And I'm really at peace with that. As much as I'm going to hate it, I have to keep my eye on the prize. I know He will use this for His Glory. And there's no better place to be than in His will. He never promised days without pain and suffering but He did promise to never forsake us.

Day 60

"Yet the Lord longs to be gracious to you; therefore he will rise up to show you compassion. For the Lord is a God of justice. Blessed are all who wait for him!"
Isaiah 30:18

On our way to Moffitt for a full day of scans.

I have to journal about this wig thing. At the beginning of all this, I saw a TikTok of a very young girl with breast cancer who had a wig made from her own hair. I saved the video but hoped I would never need it. Now that chemo has a starring role, I found the video and got the information from it to have a wig made from my hair. I researched what it would take: time/effort/money. Since things are moving so rapidly, I will likely be bald by next weekend. A wig made from my own hair would take 3 months and $2,000. I was deflated; that's so much money and a long time to wait. So, I put it out of my mind. Then my dear friend called to say she was buying me a wig, and she won't take no for an answer. I nearly collapsed. She was so excited to do this for me. I could barely speak enough to thank her. I did not want to accept such an incredibly extravagant gift, but God had clearly laid it on her heart to do this. For now, I plan to order a human hair wig and donate my hair to someone else. That way, I can have a wig quickly, but my hair will not go to waste. I'm not finished researching, but there are several options that are close to my hair color, and I would be able to style it just like I'm used to. I could barely sleep from the excitement of being able to look more like myself and maybe even feel like myself. I haven't ordered it yet, but it only takes about a week to arrive, so I will wait until things progress a little further.

Sitting in the waiting room, listening and watching. It's entertaining, to say the least. Especially being with Chad. He notices everything, but you wouldn't know it. I, on the other hand, eavesdrop on every conversation around me. It's amazing the things people talk about. I'm constantly saying, "OMG, did you hear that?" Or "Can you believe that guy?" And Chad is oblivious. He misses unbelievable confessions. I just listened to a guy that sounded like he was a slowed-down record player. He told the story of how he loves reefer and he rolls the best joints you've ever seen. He started having trouble rolling and felt like something was wrong. So he went to the ER and they did a CT scan to find he had 5 tumors in his brain. I see another younger man, with a man's name, carrying a purse, his purse. I hear an old veteran say, "What global warming? We got eight feet of snow in Buffalo!" Others sit and moan and groan and huff and puff. I'm clearly too young to be here; I don't fit in except for my old lady name Kathleen. I wonder what they think I'm here for and I'm sure they wonder who this burley hunk is sitting next to me. Signs are posted everywhere to silence your phone, yet phones are continuously going off loudly while nurses call out names that no one can hear or understand. Reefer dude thinks every nurse calls his name. No one has called his name. Some of the people here are so pitiful. Weak and bald and frail.

They've called "Kathleen" 3 times now, none of them were Rader. They were old ladies. I knew I had an old lady's name. Finally, it was my turn; I had a bone scan and a CT. Both went fine. They always give you a warm blanket and a fluffy pillow. I got tucked in nicely and tightly like a burrito. I thought I would be able to doze off a bit. But my nurse was pretty boisterous. She had a very deep voice and had a burst of nervous laughter after every few sentences. I never knew what was so funny, and then I realized she couldn't help it, almost like a tick. She'd say "How are you doing in there? You have about 5 more minutes, HAHAHAHAHA. Then I'd close my eyes again for 5 minutes and " Alrighty, now we're going to scan your ribs, HAHAHA-HAHA." She was very kind and caring, but I felt guilty not laughing along. Everyone has been extremely nice, and the valet people greet you like a celebrity when you arrive, even though we drive the old '06 Tundra. The cafeteria ladies call you 'precious' and 'sweetie'. It's a very nice atmosphere, given all the sick people. All of the receptionists seem so happy to be there, which makes me grateful for their hiring process.

Once we got home, I was wiped out, so I took a nice nap, and then Chad and I took a walk with Theo. The weather has been so nice, I'd much rather have to wear a coat than get sweaty. This week, my stamina seems much better already. I'm going to keep walking every day, so I don't lose any strength that I've gotten back. On the way home from the scans, I was called and asked to be part of a research study that would help future chemo patients. Of course, I can do that. It's a series of surveys about how I feel before, during and after treatment. Tonight, my oncologist called to say the board met and agreed that radiation alone, without further lymph node surgery, would give me the best chance at not developing lymphedema, so following three months of chemo, I'll begin a series of radiation. All of this reminds me of a childhood song, 'He's still workin' on me'.

Day 61

"As a father has compassion on his children, so the Lord has compassion on those who fear him"
Psalm 103:13

"Have kids," they say. "It'll be fun!" they say. Well, 'they' are clueless. Kids will literally kill you. I love my girls more than life itself, but I am fully convinced that if we were given a 30-second glimpse of the emotions we would experience during parenthood, I think the birth rate would drop drastically. The good far outweighs the bad. But the bad can suck the lifeblood out of you. Once you have kids, you will never sleep again, not like you did before. You'll never have privacy. There's always some emergency when you're buck naked and they come barging in. You'd think they would've learned by now. She's scarred herself several times by coming into my room when I'm walking out of the shower. And yes, Harper, your boobs will hang this low one day too! (From having kids) That's what you get for entering without knocking! I usually just wait until they're at school to use the bathroom because as soon as you sit down, "MOM!!!!!." And it could be that someone is bleeding to death or they forgot to have me sign a school paper. The screams are the same. You can love someone and want to kill them at the same time. It's unbelievable what the little people can do to you. My girls are precious, of course! They are healthy, beautiful, and smart, but they also have more drama than Young & The Restless. It's always something. It seems like they can't both be happy at the same time, so when one is easy-going, the other is a nightmare. We all three usually get our periods around the same time, so that's always fun. The amount of money we spend on feminine products is outrageous.

Parenthood carries so much responsibility and that's where the stress comes from. You've never worried so much about someone else's diet and bowel movements in your life. Is their headache from dehydration or a tumor? When's the last time they had a decent meal? You worry, are they happy, are they a good friend, are they spiritually fulfilled, are they going to make it to college, what job will they have and on and on. Exhausting. Not to mention all of the milestones. Kindergarten, middle school, high school, driving. It would be easier not to care; I've known parents like that. I never thought I'd have to worry about my kid losing her butt cheek from a dog bite! But that's exactly what Presley came home with today. Two giant puncture wounds in her butt cheek from a friend's large breed dog. She spent the night with her bestie last night, and they played 'manhunt' in the woods. I guess the dog was excited. I don't know. But do you think my brilliant kid thought, "Oh! I should probably disinfect that and call my mom."? Nope! Or better yet, how about even telling the mom who owned the dog? Nope! That's another thing they don't tell you about kids. They don't come with common sense. At all. I mean zero. You have to teach every single bit. It's mentally draining, like there are tiny leeches attached to your brain at all times, just sucking any remaining brain matter left. But I love being a mom. I really do! Like I said, you want to kill them while simultaneously stepping in front of a bullet for them. Crazy. I mean, who knows, maybe I could be locked up for these thoughts. But any mother honest with herself has thought these things too.

So right now, instead of worrying about chemo, I'm worried my kid will lose one buttock, which would make it extremely hard to sit on the toilet. I swear, as I'm disinfecting her wounds, she is giggling. I told her it wouldn't be funny when they amputated it! It's a legit dog bite, not a little scratch. It's always something like this with these kids. Makes me wonder what God thinks of me. He has to get frustrated when I don't use the common sense He gave me or I don't go down the path He has clearly set for me. Yet He loves me so much and I can never lose that love. AND He DIED for Me! He would do it all again if I were the only human on earth. That's how special I am to Him. So how can I worry about chemo or butt cheeks when the creator of the universe is my loving Father.

Day 62

*"And he said unto them, Go ye into all the world, and
preach the gospel to every creature."*
Mark 16:15

This morning pastor continued on the series of being fearless in
our faith. Fearlessly obedient. He said delayed obedience is disobedience. Wow. That really got me. I wrote a few days ago about my lack
of boldness in sharing my faith. About a month into my diagnosis, I
felt God nudge me to share my journal with a specific person. I basically told Him no. I remember it very clearly. I cried because I knew I
was saying no to the God of the universe. But I have only shared my
story with others that would understand me and that would understand Him. I only shared it with people I was comfortable sharing it
with. I had friends tell me that my journal helped them in some way,
and I felt encouraged and looked forward to hearing what God had to
say in my situation. But I felt like some people might not get it. So,
I disobeyed. And the moment passed. And I promised Him I would
listen next time if He would just give me another chance. I wouldn't
worry about what others thought because all I was called to do was
share my experience. He would handle the rest. And weeks later, I felt
again that He wanted me to share my journal with another person,
and again, I questioned Him. I tried to tell myself it wasn't the Holy
Spirit nudging me. It was just a passing thought I had. But I know
better.

I felt the nudging continue. Again, I disobeyed. Even though I
write this journal for myself, it has helped my friends to know exactly where I stand and maybe even encouraged them in their own
struggles. And by not sharing with those two people, I may have kept
them from knowing God the way I do. I hope and pray that's not the
case. God doesn't need me to fulfill His will, but He does expect me

to obey, especially when I have surrendered myself to be used by Him. I have to work on my boldness in sharing what Christ has done for me. I am not ashamed of Him or my faith. My disobedience comes from my lack of seeing His vision in using me. I feel inadequate, and I know better about that, too. So I have to find the root of what's causing my insecurities so that the next time He directs me, I will listen. If He even bothers to ask me. How many times do you ask your child to do something before you give up? I know that any discouragement I feel is from the devil. He doesn't want God to get the glory for working in my life. I know all of these things. But that is a stronghold I am definitely battling. I'm embarrassed to write this and have people I love see my shortcomings, but this is really something I have to overcome; otherwise, what am I even fighting all this for? What's the whole point of being #godsfave and not sharing that?

Day 63

"Your word is a lamp for my feet, a light on my path."
Psalm 119:105

All of my scans came back today, showing that the cancer has not spread any further. So, I will start chemo as scheduled tomorrow and follow up with the radiologist next week to determine how much radiation he thinks I will need. I'm very at peace with whatever is to come. I've had lots of phone calls, messages, visitors and gifts today to remind me how many people are still praying for me. Dina brought a huge anti-nausea kit so I could be fully prepared. Brenda brought me medical-grade puke bags. An edible arrangement was delivered (not the edible brownies with marijuana), but I wouldn't turn that away and one of my clients brought dinner and a care package. I continue to receive cards in the mail every day, and it's so uplifting to have reminders that people care, even two months later. I am immeasurably blessed and all I want is for my children to feel the same way and know what I know about our Heavenly Father.

Day 64

"Jesus looked at them and said, 'With man this is
impossible, but with God all things are possible.'"
Matthew 19:26

It's go time. I'm ready. Or I thought I was ready. I don't know what I was expecting. But it wasn't this. I've tried to take in all the details, but there are so many. And now I've been given a lot of Benadryl, so things are a little fuzzy. We arrived at 7:30am this morning and I had labs done immediately. Then, we were directed to the infusion center on the fifth floor. Small little cubicles with a privacy curtain, a recliner, and a tiny little chair for my guest. When the nurse saw Chad, she said she'd be right back with a comfier(bigger) chair. So far, I was ok. It wasn't bad, right? Why do people get upset when they hear 'chemo'? A lady from the study I am participating in dropped by for me to fill a tube with my saliva, gross, but not bad. My nurse began hooking up my pre-meds.

The pharmacist came in, let's call him McDreamy, to explain all the side effects. Everyone is wearing a mask so that he could have had huge bucky beaver teeth behind his mask. But I don't think so. He carefully explained each medication and its possible effects on the body. I had a hard time keeping my emotions in check when he was explaining, not because of his crystal blue eyes but because of the reality of these drugs and my situation. I held it together. I had read my Chemo for Dummies booklet already, but it helped to hear it, too. The first major side effect is 'DEATH,' that's if you're given too much, of course. But I've never had chemo, so how much is TOO much? After that, it's 'You'll wish you were dead' symptoms. Mouth sores, bone pain, dry mouth, constipation, diarrhea, hair loss, weight gain, water retention and pretty much anything unpleasant you can think of. Then, the pharmacist asked if I was doing cold therapy. What? My doctor explained it to me, but I thought it was optional.

Cold therapy is to help prevent neuropathy in your fingers and toes. They strap ice packs to your hands and feet for 15 minutes before the infusion, during the infusion, and 15 minutes after, so roughly two hours. The cold constricts the blood vessels flow to these areas to keep the chemo from reaching all the way to the tips, resulting in less chance for neuropathy. So, when my nurse placed my hands and feet into ice bags, I was not happy. I thought I would be able to curl up in the recliner and doze. How can you possibly get comfortable with your extremities frozen? I wouldn't be able to use my hands for two hours. No reading, writing, or scrolling. So whatever, I pulled up my granny panties and let my extremities freeze.

The first bag of chemo is almost ready to drip. If I have any weird feelings at all, I am to buzz them immediately. So, we dim the lights and start to settle as much as you can with freezing toes. My Nurse begins the drip. She makes sure I'm comfortable and goes out of the room. I immediately start to feel hot; I feel my face flushing, my chest gets painfully tight, and my nose and throat swell shut. I'm having trouble breathing. I sit up quickly and look at Chad. I don't feel good, and then BAM! I cannot breathe. I push the call button, and 4 nurses rush in. The nurse had barely just walked away from me. They immediately shut off the drip and started administering concoctions into my IV. My throat begins to open, and I gasp for air. They start asking me questions. They were talking amongst themselves calmly but seriously about my visible symptoms, saying how red my face was and I looked strange. I could feel my lips swelling. Just four minutes into chemo, and I can't breathe; I am scared shitless. How can I do this? I started to cry. I was terrified.

I began to get relief from my symptoms very quickly from all the meds they were shooting into me. I got so sleepy from the Benadryl. I just wanted to stop the whole thing. I can't do this. This isn't for the faint of heart. They wanted to monitor me for thirty minutes without treatment to make sure my symptoms were clear. Then, they would start it back at half the rate. So now my time will be increased because it'll take longer to empty the bag. Good times! My symptoms slowly reversed, except now I was so sleepy and couldn't get comfortable with freezing fingers and toes. I really thought I'd come in, get hooked up, drip for six hours and go. And maybe the next appointments will go that way, but I will worry about that happening again from here on out. I really felt sorry for myself, and for others that have had to do this or are about to. It really is scary to think about these drugs and what they are doing. If they're killing cancer what else does it kill? It's not like me to stay in the valley very long, so I know in a few hours from now, or the latest tomorrow, I will be better. But right now, the lump in my throat is back (not cancer), and I want to have a pity party for myself.

I finished the first bag and the ice bags were removed. What a relief! I can curl up in my chair and write *You Don't Need Headlights to Shine*, at least. When your hands are in ice bags, all you can do is sit and stare into oblivion. I don't even care about the chatter going on around me. I want to go home. I want my life BC (before cancer), But then I wouldn't have these awesome yellow hospital socks with grippers on the bottom to take home, and I wouldn't be so close to my heavenly father. I know He has gone before me, and I know He is with me, and I am no longer fearful, but I don't want to do it anymore. I hope that by writing this, I can look back after my next treatment and think, 'Wow! What a whiny baby! It's not that bad!'

So I'm on bag number two now, and there are no ice packs. But I still can't sleep because I have to pee so badly, and I'm not asking my nurse to unhook me again because I've gone to the bathroom 20 times already. She is so kind and says it's not a big deal, but I see all the things she has to do so that I can tinkle. When this bag is finished, I will go. And next time, I'm wearing Depends.

Another plus is that the food cart lady brought me a chicken Caesar wrap, and it was delish! I have had more of an appetite this last week so I have been eating more than string cheese and orange juice. I actually gained three pounds, but I'm bloated, and the Tweedle Ds weigh at least that. And my friend brought me her famous 'death by chocolate' dessert, and I may have eaten the whole thing, but I'm not sure. I've been so steady with my weight loss I'd hate to have a setback.

That would really be upsetting. So I'm still claiming 42 pounds down since June.

It's been hours since we got home. I wasn't able to sleep, but I rested. I'm still emotional about what happened. I cry every time I think about it, but I am alright. I'm not worried about it happening again. It was just so scary. I have 3 weeks before I have to go back, so I will use that time to focus on staying well and doing everything my doctors tell me to do, especially McDreamy.

Day 65

"The Lord is the stronghold of my life—of whom shall I be afraid? When the wicked advance against me to devour me, it is my enemies and my foes who will stumble and fall. Though an army besiege me, my heart will not fear; though war break out against me, even then I will be confident. One thing I ask from the Lord, this only do I seek: that I may dwell in the house of the Lord all the days of my life, to gaze on the beauty of the Lord and to seek him in his temple. For in the day of trouble he will keep me safe in his dwelling; he will hide me in the shelter of his sacred tent and set me high upon a rock. Then my head will be exalted above the enemies who surround me; at his sacred tent I will sacrifice with shouts of joy; I will sing and make music to the Lord. Hear my voice when I call, Lord; be merciful to me and answer me. My heart says of you, "Seek his face!" Your face, Lord, I will seek. Do not hide your face from me, do not turn your servant away in anger; you have been my helper. Do not reject me or forsake me, God my Savior. Though my father and mother forsake me, the Lord will receive me. Teach me your way, Lord; lead me in a straight path because of my oppressors. Do not turn me over to the desire of my foes, for false witnesses rise up against me, spouting malicious accusations. I remain confident of this: I will see the goodness of the Lord in the land of the living. Wait for the Lord; be strong and take heart and wait for the Lord."
Psalm 27:1-14

I woke up to the feeling of morning sickness. I could hardly brush my teeth. I drank water and fixed my coffee like normal. I don't feel bad exactly, just not myself. I'm wearing a patch on my arm that injects medicine. It feels like a rubber band popping your arm. Fun times. It also flashes a green light every 5 seconds. Chad said I looked like a landing strip in bed last night. Just something else for us to giggle about. He didn't think it was too funny that I mentioned Mc-Dreamy in my journal, though. I know for a fact that if McDreamy had been female, we would've had a discussion about her dreaminess, too. So sorry, bud! There's got to be something nice to look at in that place. Besides, I probably am old enough to be his mother. We're getting to the age where all of these caregivers are much younger than us. So let this old lady have a little fun. He wouldn't want a bald lady with no nipples anyway! I'm not bald yet, of course, but it's on the way.

I ordered my wig today. It should be here in a week, and then Krysta will cut my hair to be donated. I know it won't be easy, but I am getting used to the idea of it. And Chad isn't worried about it at all. I'm sure if his younger self were told his future wife would be 100 lbs. heavier than when you met her, she wouldn't have nipples, and she would be bald for a little bit, he would've run like a scalded dog (something his mom always says). But he's been wonderful. Not that I am surprised, but he never shows emotion other than caveman emotions (grunts and hisses). So, it's nice that he's been honest with me about how he feels during this whole process. Enough about him. I need his head to fit through the door.

I've had to start putting my phone on *Do Not Disturb* if I need to rest. I usually don't ever do that in case one of the girls needs me. I was able to get a little nap and feel somewhat better. I don't see how I could work feeling this way. Lots of people do, but I am not sure how they do it. I'm sure when it's time for me to work again, God will make it a seamless transition. I try not to worry about how it's going to work out because I can't imagine His timeline. I have another month before I am cleared to work and that includes one more chemo during that time. I guess it will depend on how I am handling all of it. And how good my wig looks, or if I'm confident enough to just wear a cap. Next week, I will see about the radiation schedule, so that will also take up time. It's hard to think I could possibly not work a regular schedule for six months. But life has a way of taking turns you could never imagine, but at every turn, God has been there with me and never failed. This is by far the sharpest turn in the road, but I've had the most peace on this ride. It really is such a relief to 'Let go and let God," as the saying goes.

Day 66

"Seek the Lord while he may be found; call on him while he is near. Let the wicked forsake their ways and the unrighteous their thoughts. Let them turn to the Lord, and he will have mercy on them, and to our God, for he will freely pardon. 'For my thoughts are not your thoughts, neither are your ways my ways,' declares the Lord. 'As the heavens are higher than the earth, so are my ways higher than your ways and my thoughts than your thoughts. As the rain and the snow come down from heaven, and do not return to it without watering the earth and making it bud and flourish, so that it yields seed for the sower and bread for the eater, so is my word that goes out from my mouth: It will not return to me empty, but will accomplish what I desire and achieve the purpose for which I sent it. You will go out in joy and be led forth in peace; the mountains and hills will burst into song before you, and all the trees of the field will clap their hands. Instead of the thornbush will grow the juniper, and instead of briers the myrtle will grow. This will be for the Lord's renown, for an everlasting sign, that will endure forever.'"
Isaiah 55:6-13

I was born on my grandmother's birthday. I was her first grand-child born on her special day. My mom cried because she wanted me to have my own day, but it made my grandparents so proud. Granny and I were a lot more alike than I'd like to admit. We had our share of disagreements over the years. Now that she's gone, I can appreciate the similarities. She was stubborn (I am not) I'm just describing her. I get my love of antiques from her. She always pulled me aside and would give me things she knew I'd appreciate. I have her high school graduation picture framed in my living room, where she graduated with none other than the great Johnny Cash in Dyess, Arkansas. I have her high school ring and her pearls and many, many dishes and glassware that I treasure. I like to use them instead of hiding them away. Of course, that means things can get chipped or broken, but I get to enjoy them instead of putting them away in some cabinet.

I've been very flu-like and achy, even more so today, so I decided to take an Epsom bath. I store my salts in one of Granny's antique jars beside the tub. Of all days, I dropped the lid, and it shattered. The lump I've had in my throat all day burst. I'll never find another lid for that jar. They don't even make stuff like that anymore. And I feel so stupid being sad about it. All these meds have my emotions going crazy. I'm trying very hard not to get too low in the valley or stay too long. I know it's normal, just not for me. So, I sit here and soak my bones and catch a glimpse of the twins. I still haven't looked full on. They're not too bad. Normally, a soak in the tub wouldn't have to be very full to get them wet; they are high above the water line. That actually makes me laugh. Laughing really is the best medicine. And while I can't see what God's doing in this mess, I still trust in Him. Who knows? Maybe when I feel better, I will run across another jar on one of my antiquing ventures because I know I'm #Godsfavorite, and maybe even granny will guide me to one because even though she never said it out loud, I was her favorite too.

Day 67

*"Consider it pure joy, my brothers and sisters, whenever you
face trials of many kinds, because you know that the testing
of your faith produces perseverance. Let perseverance finish
its work so that you may be mature and complete, not
lacking anything."*
James 1:2-4

♪ Oh, well, my hands are shaky, and my knees are weak. I can't seem to stand on my own two feet♪♪ Not because I'm in love. Chemo side effects. Today is much better, though, but I woke up to a new thing; I think my implant has flipped. My bad boob was really sore this morning, and as I felt around, I got pretty freaked out. Then I looked. Bad idea. It's misshapen and ripply. I emailed my plastic surgeon right away. They wanted pictures, of course. So, I got my personal photographer out of bed. "Hey honey, can you take some pictures of my boobs?" The man had never moved so fast in his life.

Doc is pretty sure it has changed position somehow. There is nothing I could've done; it can happen. I was just getting used to them and now I'm deformed again. I have appointments next week anyway, so they will see me to see if they can reposition it in the clinic. Hmmm, that should be interesting. I'm fine with waiting until June when I have all the final tweaks done, except this is not comfortable. They suggested I wear a bra to help support it. Look, not wearing a bra has been the highlight of all this. Whatever. I can handle it.

My emotions seem more in check today. I guess the pain had a way of making me weepy, which I absolutely hate. I don't do the damsel in distress act very much. I'm pretty independent. Cancer has shown me that I can't always be that. I've let people bring food for me and I haven't felt bad about it one bit. I've had visitors see me with no makeup and my PJs, no chin hairs, though. That's where I draw the line. I think I'd have to be in a coffin to let that happen. Tomorrow has to be the downhill slope to this week. I'm getting cabin fever and I've got to go somewhere. My dad got new baby chicks yesterday, so we went to see them tonight, and that was enough adventure for today.

In all of my studies, I follow some incredible Pastors. I'm learning about how God works when we are in the valley. There's a lot of vegetation in a valley, usually streams and new growth. Not much usually can survive at the top of a mountain. So when we get down low, God is able to pour into us because we have nowhere else to turn. I have always known this is how God works, but I'm sad to say I've never been in a position that forced me to grow. I mean, I'm glad I haven't had major trials, but at the same time, I was stagnant and didn't really know. We've had minor life things, careers, kids, and normal stresses, but nothing that took me to my knees. Now I can see He's up to something and I'm also learning that He won't tell you what it is. You have to seek it. He wants to know that you really want whatever He is working on. If He just gives it to me, I'll just treat it like my kids treat me when I constantly give them things. 'New shoes? Oh sure, Mom, they're ok 'A trip to the mall just because? Not really in the mood to shop.' So He lets us get way down and then offers up His Kingdom, and as His children, it already belongs to us, but it's meant to be enjoyed now, not just in heaven. All He asks is that we seek it. And while I'm hoping and praying the darkest days are behind me, I'm also a realist. I will continue to seek whatever it is He has in store because whenever I'm done with all this, I don't plan on going back to being stagnant.

Day 68

Yes, my soul, find rest in God: my hope comes from him.
Psalm 62:5

I felt good enough to venture out today. The bone pain has subsided and I have some energy. Chad got us up and took us to brunch and furniture shopping. It was nice to have a normal day with the kids too.

The twins aren't exactly twins anymore since the bad boob has flipped. We now have Tweedle D, who has behaved appropriately, and we have Sponge Blob Square Pants, who is all over the place and not even in the pineapple under the sea. If Sponge Blob doesn't get fixed next week or ends up staying in Square Pants, I will have it tattooed with his big googly eyes and pants and a tie because I'll never see it any other way. In the beginning, I told the doctor anything would be an improvement, and I wasn't picky. He insisted that I would care in the end, and I guess I do. I have friends who still haven't had reconstruction surgery two years later, and here I was with round, firm, high breasts! Life was looking up! Until Sponge Blob showed up. I wasn't even allowed to watch that show as a kid. Now he's sitting on my chest. At least I can joke about it now. My emotions are more stable today. Yesterday, it had me on edge. Just another bump in the road, which I'm sure won't be the last. It's not tender like it was, either, so that's good.

So Sponge Blob may be part of God's plan for my earthly body, and if that's so, I will continue to look forward to my heavenly body that I'm sure will most resemble Cindy Crawford.

Day 69

"God is mighty, but despises no one;
he is mighty, and firm in his purpose."
Job 36:5

The four days following chemo, I had specific pain pills, but after day four, they didn't mention anything. So when I woke up from my nap with pelvic pain, I was a little shocked, but it was bearable. Walking around seemed to help at first. We decided to go for a bite to eat instead of takeout out and I thought moving around would help. I still didn't take anything for pain. As we left the house, the pain would come in breathtaking waves. I would cringe at the surprise of it. Trying to hide that kind of discomfort from your family is not easy. It feels exactly like a vaginal birth. Like when the pelvis begins to separate to allow the baby to move down. Exactly that same pain. So naturally, I try to breathe through it, and it passes. The intensity is indescribable; at this point, I would ask for an epidural. I have no idea how someone can endure this feeling long-term. I would love to just lay on the floor and scream, but what would that help? It's excruciating. I haven't really had much nausea this week, but I could actually vomit from this pain. Now that I'm back at home I'm sitting in the tub with good old Epsom. It's not really touching it. I took the meds from my previous days and emailed my doctors about what else they'd like me to do. Hopefully, I'll hear from them bright and early tomorrow.

This morning, Rachel sent me a song by Natalie Grant called More Than Anything. It was so powerful, and I let the words wash over me; I'd never heard it before. But it has been my prayer all along. This pain is temporary; my Jesus is forever, and I want Him more than healing. I want to stop treatment right now and give up. I just don't see how I can withstand it; supposedly, it will get more painful. But I have to keep going at this point and I'm not sure what that looks like.

Day 70

*"But you, Lord, are a shield around me, my glory, the One
who lifts my head high."*
Psalm 3:3

Me and Epsom reflecting on last night. I need to document for
my future self how bad it was. My mental state wasn't worn down; it
was the physical pain I couldn't handle. Almost delirious with pain.
But it's easy to see that it wouldn't take much more for my mental state to follow. I just can't fathom how anyone could go through
anything this hard without support. I ended up calling my nurse last
night and we figured out some relief and how to prevent it from getting so bad in the future. The medicine I have to build my blood cell
count causes severe bone pain. So, I need to take it to keep my blood
cells growing. You won't find it in medical books yet, but certain allergy meds happen to fight bone pain; that is part of my regimen. How
long could someone survive that kind of discomfort without knowing
an end or without hope? I can see how easy it would be to give up. I'm
grateful for my huge support system. I know there are people who do
this all alone and I can't even begin to imagine how they get through
it. While I hope to never feel that pain again, I have to remind myself
it was like childbirth without drugs, and today I am so much better.
I'm tired from fighting against it for hours. I feel beaten up. But I'm
ready to have a more normal day tomorrow, even if it involves meeting my radiologist.

I still haven't gotten used to sixteen inches of scars across my
chest, but I think it's better than seeing Sponge Blob. I shouldn't have
complained about the scars when I have to carry him around now.
He's completely loose in there, living his best life, sometimes in my
armpit but never in the pineapple under the sea where he belongs. I
have to laugh at something to keep from crying. This is by far not the
end of the world or my life. Just a small blip in time that I can look

back on and remember God's goodness and favor in my darkness. Our bills are paid, our stomachs are full, we can get to every place we need to go and even still have fun. It hasn't all been bad. I never thought I could sit around and not work for several months. I couldn't even close down for Covid six weeks. But look at me now? God has a way and no one ever could see it coming.

Day 71

"By wisdom a house is built,
and through understanding it is established"
Proverbs 24:3

Twenty-five radiation treatments. That's what the doctor ordered. I'm writing this with a throbbing headache, dry mouth, heartburn, chest and back pain. And that's just from one chemo. Radiation has another set of crap. I sat this morning in front of my very competent doctors and nurses, who explained very clearly and compassionately the reasons for my next chapter of treatment. I was in a very present state of mind. At the onset of diagnosis, I was in a fog of information and disbelief, but now I am accustomed to the reality and can really focus. Looking into my sweet doctor's eyes, that's all I could see with her mask on; I focused on the terrible things she was gently telling me. She is so young; how can she be so smart? Of course, she isn't telling me I will die, but that I will very much live. The part I get upset about is what side effects will I live with? I have no idea how long I have left. I mean, I could expire tomorrow if that's God's plan, but realistically, I should have decades, and some of the side effects just got to me. I'm too young to just go decades with no repercussions from all this poison. This is so negative to write. I know that, but as I sit here hurting, I don't see how I will ever not hurt again in some way.

Chad has always called me an old lady, and I am. I'm proud of it. I love my early bedtime, my sensible shoes, my chic yet comfortable attire and I will never give up my seat belt pillow, but I like having the feeling of being young. Now I feel old and I'm scared I always will. Everyone is different, of course; that's how all of these conversations with doctors start, but here are some common effects you may notice. Chemo was scary to hear about, of course, with the hair loss and bone pain. Radiation isn't something I really thought too much about so it surprised me that I got emotional. The area to be radiated includes all of the lymphatic system that would have connected to my right breast. My neck, ribs and underarm will be precisely treated. It's amazing, really, what and how they do it. She described the changes in my skin, my lungs and ribs and maybe a smidge of my heart would get radiation. My ribs will never be as strong in that area again. There's nothing to be done about that. There's a chance I could develop cancer in this area as well. 1/1000 after 10 years. It's just mind-boggling; I'm doing one thing to cure a thing that can cause the same thing to come back. All a means to an end. The motto is to cure me once and for all this time around and that means pulling out all the stops. I get it, I really do and I'm all in. I just hope and pray when my future self reads this in 2033 that, I can laugh at how barbaric this all was because there's a pill we can pop to make it all go away. I'm going to get some fresh air and clear this negativity out of my mind and maybe later I'll like myself again.

When we built our house a few years ago we stopped by every day to see the progress. Some days, it would be a giant mess, and it was hard to see how the house would come together in the end. I know that's what God is working on in my heart. Some days, it's a mess, and I can't see what He's doing, but there is progress being made. He's rebuilding me. So, I will trust the process and look forward to the finished product.

Day 72

"Obey your earthly masters in everything; and do it, not
only when their eye is on you and to curry their favor,
but with sincerity of heart and reverence for the Lord.
Whatever you do, work at it with all your heart, as
working for the Lord, not for human masters, since you
know that you will receive an inheritance from the Lord
as a reward. It is the Lord Christ you are serving. Anyone
who does wrong will be repaid for their wrongs, and there
is no favoritism."
Colossians 3:22-25

Me, Epsom, Sponge Blob and The Judds. That's all it takes, and I am renewed until bedtime, that is. I have small bursts of energy where I run around and do tidbits of laundry or cleaning before I have to take a little rest. My mind has big plans every day to do many things, but then ol' granny kicks in and I have to sit down. I'm technically cleared to do most anything; I think they're worried about what I do for a living, continuously or strenuously; they haven't said I could do that yet, and I don't see how I could. It would be one client and a two-hour nap at this point. I know I'll get there eventually; I can't stand not seeing my clients for this long. Over the years, God has blessed me with AMAZING clients whom I call my friends. It's so special to be entwined into people's lives at first because they like how you do their hair, but they stay because of the relationship you build. We solve the world's problems behind my chair. We repair marriages and discipline other people's children and plan the most important days in our lives. I get to cry and laugh hysterically every day with my friends, all while getting paid.

I miss talking about life with my people, especially this section of life. I'm missing weddings, funerals, babies, birthdays. Texting isn't the same as getting all the juicy details of the crazy sisters-in-law or the nosy moms or jailbird neighbors. I'm nosy by nature, and in this job, all you have to do is ask, and they will tell. I've gotten unsolicited information as well. I must have an invisible sign on my forehead that says, 'Tell me your deepest, darkest secrets, and I'll pretend it doesn't faze me.' All jokes aside, I love it. We all just want to connect with someone and feel normal. And that's what I love about my job. When I get back, there will be so many untold stories to catch up on. Not many know about Sponge Bob, but hopefully, he'll be back under the sea by then, and me and the twins can get back to slingin' hair like the good ol' days.

Day 73

"Surely your goodness and love will follow me
all the days of my life,
and I will dwell in the house of the Lord forever."
Psalm 23:6

I met with some of my plastics team this morning to introduce SpongeBlob to them officially. Since he moved in last week, they've only seen pictures. And since becoming a doctor myself (16 seasons of Grey's Anatomy) my diagnosis was correct. My implant completely flipped 360°. Implants are dome-shaped, flat on the back, with a rounded top. The middle of the back has a tiny valve in the center. As the resident was rounding 3rd base with SpongeBlob (maybe second base, depending on how fast you like to move), she explained that the flat part of the implant would give my breast the square pants shape I was now seeing. She was amazed at how maneuverable Blob was. For a moment, I saw stars (not Patrick), and it kinda hurt. I haven't aggressively squeezed the twins at all, but she assured me they wouldn't rupture and I could not damage them in any way. Decidedly, the pocket of skin that is left is too big for the size of the implant now that the swelling is gone.

So, as I expected, I will have another surgery at the very end to add a bigger implant and fat grafting. Chad is thrilled of course, me, eh. I can't have Blob doing his thing forever; it's quite annoying, but the thought of another surgery is blah. I was told a one-and-done philosophy wasn't likely, but of course, I had hoped. I had hoped for just a mastectomy and nothing else ever. But I digress. With the Superbowl approaching, the resident and I joked that I could do a few Super Bowl halftime tricks like the infamous Janet Jackson when JT ripped off her top to expose a star-covered nipple. I could use Patrick the starfish to cover my non-nipple. Remember when that Janet Jackson thing was such a scandal? Now look at us, Janet's little boobie is the least of our concerns. My boob really is more of a circus sideshow, anyway.

Today, I felt the most normal since my surgery. My energy was up all day until about 7 p.m. when the body aches started to kick in. That's when I get with Epsom.

My appetite is back, which I know is good right now, but I'm worried I'll gain back all the weight I've worked so hard to get off since June. Most people lose weight with cancer, but knowing me, I'll be on *1000-Lbs Sisters* with a bald head.

I want to remember how good I feel today, ten days after chemo #1. I'm reading a book about a woman who went through breast cancer and so much more than one human could ever endure. Her experience is so parallel to mine in so many ways as she discusses the growth in her faith. She's a Christian like me her whole life, but cancer found a way of bringing her closer to God than she could ever have imagined. She hates cancer, but she's grateful for the journey because, without it, she wouldn't have that relationship now. That's exactly how I feel. It sounds sick to say that cancer can be a blessing, but isn't that what God does? He turns everything bad into good for His glory. So even on my best day, I am seeking Him as I will on my worst day, and through all of these days, His blessings will shine on me, and in turn, maybe I'll be brave enough to share it.

Day 74

*"These commandments that I give you today are to be on
your hearts. Impress them on your children.
Talk about them when you sit at home and when you walk
along the road, when you lie down and when you get up.
Tie them as symbols on your hands and bind them on your
foreheads. Write them on the doorframes of
your houses and on your gates."*
Deuteronomy 6:6-9

My energy level is holding steady. I should get better and better leading up to the next treatment. Today, I was gone all day with two of my girlfriends, pedis, coffee, shopping and lunch. I had enough stamina the whole time and then we had friends come over for dinner with their kids and I was still standing! It's so nice to have two normal days in a row! I also need to document that sometime around last Tuesday, I noticed my right leg started to get these tiny sores. At first, it looked like ant bites. I did not mess with them (I'm pretty infamous for playing esthetician) or pick at them because Dr. Hoover had a fit over a pimple I had on my chest weeks ago. She got all freaked out that it could get an infection and lose my implant. So I honestly left them alone except to clean and medicate them as she instructed me to do about my chest pimple. A few days later, there were more, and they were extremely sore, swollen and oozing. It's pretty gross and embarrassing. I'm treating them on my own with my self-acquired MD TV knowledge and if they don't get better, I'll call the real Dr.

Day 75

"Rejoice always, pray continually, give thanks in all circumstances; for this is God's will for you in Christ Jesus."
1 Thessalonians 5:16-18

I am continuing to receive the kindest, most thoughtful gifts, sometimes from the most unexpected people. I had no idea the convenient things they made for mastectomy and chemotherapy patients. I got a few mastectomy pillows and button-up tops that had pockets for my drains. These gifts ended up being lifesavers and the people that sent them had to have done research that I didn't even think to do. Yesterday, I got a cozy zip-up hoodie with a note to "stay warm during chemo." How incredibly thoughtful, but then I tried it on and found that the sleeves have zippers running up and down so that I can actually wear it during chemo with my IV! Genius! I had flowers and a cookie cake on my front porch when I came home, too. Just the nicest sentiments still pouring in 75 days later. My cup runneth over this entire time. My heart is so full and I have to figure out what I am supposed to do with it. There are people who don't have this kind of support and it makes me sad. Getting ready for Valentine's date night since I probably won't be "going out" very much in the near future. My hair is definitely coming out. I just touch it and strands fall. As I curl each section, I make a pile of the hair that falls. It's significant but not astonishing. I definitely never shed like this normally. So, it's here. At some point this week, I'll have to face it head-on. For now, I'll wrap it up in a bun and hope it survives church tomorrow. I'm ready for it. My beautiful wig will be here Monday, and I have silk turbans, too. I can do this. My girlfriends will be with me and we'll make a party of it. Maybe we'll have a ceremony for the beautiful hair that someone else will receive from my donation.

The sores on my leg are very painful. I sent pictures to my nurse because I had hoped they would be healed by now, so I'm anxious to see what the doctor thinks. I'm fighting against feeling sad. I'm not used to having to work at being happy, it's my usual state of mind. Pain has a way of distracting you from happiness and I don't like that.

Day 76

"On the day when I act," says the Lord Almighty, "they will be my treasured possession. I will spare them, just as a father has compassion and spares his son who serves him. And you will again see the distinction between the righteous and the wicked, between those who serve God and those who do not."
Malachi 3:7-12, 17-18

Looking back at my high school years, I sure didn't know what I had when I had it! I was a little hottie! I had no clue! If I had known then what I am facing now, then I'd have been dancing on a tabletop every weekend, appreciating the lack of joint pain. I couldn't get on top of a table now if someone paid me. Just can't lift these thunder thighs. Even now, as a chubby girl, I get compliments. I always say, "Thick in the waist, pretty in the face." My friends are the very best at hyping me up. Tell me I'm pretty, feed me tacos, and we're BFFs. So I say all this to say it's very hard watching myself deteriorate in the mirror. I am my biggest critic. On my very best day, I can pick myself apart. This morning, I clearly see my scalp on one side; I have a huge pile of hair that I keep adding to every time I touch my hair; the sores have traveled to my chest, and I have a huge crease on my face from my CPAP machine, I look frazzled. I feel like I'm falling apart. Tweedle D and Sponge Blob staring back at me, looking like cross-eyed sisters. The thought of seeing this head bald makes me nauseated. It's hard enough growing older and going through perimenopause, but this is just wrong.

I should've danced on tables when I had the chance, shook what my mama definitely gave me, a big ol' booty. But now I just shake from being cold or from my nerves. Now, when people look at me, it'll be because I look terrible. And they'll have that sad look in their eyes like, "Oh, that poor girl." I know because that's what I think when I see sickly people.

I'm currently at urgent care. I called the after-hours nurse about these sores, and she said they needed to see me. It's not fun getting poked with needles. I don't have a fear of needles, but I prefer not to watch, and I don't have the best veins, so it's never just one poke. The nurse found more sores besides the ones on my leg. I have some on my back, and I noticed one on my chest last night. Everyone is perplexed about these sores. They think they look like bug bites, but I have not been outside much and we don't have bugs in our house. The doctor asked if I had been hiking or anything outside where I would've been bitten. Good one, Doc! Do I look like someone who just goes hiking? I mean, really, you have my chart right there, lady. Look at the BMI and ask me again. She went over a million things it could be, and all of a sudden, Chad's stomach made the loudest noise. It's a gas pang; I just know it because we came here right after lunch. So the doctor probably thinks we have bed bugs and my husband is full of farts. One of those is true but still embarrassing. They gave me antibiotics and said it should not interfere with my next treatment, which was my main concern. The only way to really know it's from the chemo is if it happens again next time.

Day 77

Cast all your anxiety on him because he cares for you.
1 Peter 5:7

Today's the day. My hair is coming out too much and it's not like it will get better. I knew yesterday that I would probably have to shave it today, but emotionally, yesterday wasn't good.

Every time I touched my hair casually, or not even touching it at all it would come out in large clumps. It's everywhere: my bed, my food, and the floor. I know it will grow back and I know it will likely come back the same, just not for a very long time. I've tried to get excited about all the fun hairstyles I can try on the journey back, but I was really liking my hair lately. Isn't that how it goes? Just when your hair gets to the length you want, it's time for a trim again and you have to retrain it all over again. I put away all my styling products and tools. I'll still use my shampoo to keep my follicles cleaned. My stomach is doing little flips thinking about it. But it won't get better if I wait. And I've already decided where to donate my hair, and I have all the info ready so some sweet little baby that definitely has never done one thing in its life to deserve this horrible diagnosis can have some beautiful hair. It'll be worth it. I'll get to see how gray I really am which I never planned on finding out, but I'm learning you can't make plans like that. You can never say never.

Right now, I'm tracking my wig; I have been since 5 a.m. That UPS driver has had an eagle eye on her all day. If that little blue dot stops in one place for very long, I start looking for the customer service number.

A package just came; it's not my wig. It's so incredible, though. One of my older clients and her little church group of ladies get together every week; they pray for me daily and have sent me 30 days of cards. Each card is hand-written and labeled days 1-30 with the favorite Bible verses of the ladies in the group, along with a daily devotional. The only person I know from the group is my client. It's probably one of the most thoughtful gifts, and I've received so many. I had no idea they'd been praying except that, for the most part, I feel joy and peace, and that can only come from being prayed for by so many because some days, I can't even muster a prayer for myself. The amount of good days have far outweighed the bad and I know that's only because of God's goodness. I'm anxious for the days ahead, even though I know I shouldn't be.

It's done. Krysta came over and made little ponytails all over my head so we could salvage every inch. I could not watch her cut it, and when I finally saw it, I cried. But my beautiful wig came just in time, and it really helped the transition. It was sad, but I think I will be okay—except my head is freezing now!

Day 78

"Love must be sincere. Hate what is evil; cling to what is good. Be devoted to one another in love. Honor one another above yourselves."
Romans 12:9-10

Being bald for 12 hours, most of which I was sleeping, hasn't been too bad. After the initial shock of seeing it, I have warmed up to it quite nicely. This part is easier than the scars on my chest. I can look at my bald head already without emotion. I still don't really look at the twins. They're not twins anymore, either, so I need a new name for them. Twisted Sisters? We'll

see. But the wig arrived at just the right time. Krysta came to cut my hair at 7pm so we went out to the salon to get started before it arrived. The tracking said no later than 7pm. It was

already after 7. Before we could get started, in walks Chad with the most glorious box I'd ever seen. I should have done an "unboxing" video. This wig is incredible. Thank God it came when it did and I was able to put it on and know that I would be able to look like myself again.

Also, my sores, which I now know are boils, are healing nicely. My mom, aka Dr. June, did her research and found that while not too common, boils can be a side effect of chemo. Yay! I love being one in a million.

We ran some errands today, and by the time we were done, my wig was hot! As soon as we got in the car, I had to let my head breathe. I don't want to get my wig sweaty because I have to take her to a wig salon to have her washed and I'd like to wait as long as possible. So I'll probably wear it to church and places where I'm not working up a sweat. My wig needs a name, too; gotta think about that for a bit. Riding home without a wig, I was definitely giving Sinéad O'Connor vibes, so we had to introduce the girls to 'Nothing Compares.' I think

I might be braver than I thought about showing this bald dome. My original plan was that not a single solitary soul would see it uncovered. But I'm almost 24 hours in and I'm thinking of going over to the neighbors completely natural. The neighbors invited us over for V-Day dinner. My worry is that it will make others uncomfortable. I don't want people to feel awkward around me; Chad says they won't, and if I'm not awkward, they won't be. So we'll test it out on the unsuspecting neighbors.

On this Valentine's Day, I am so blessed. I feel like the most loved person in the whole world. Our neighbors made us an incredible steak dinner and they loved my bald head.

Day 79

"I will remember the deeds of the Lord; yes, I will remember your miracles of long ago. I will consider all your works and meditate on all your mighty deeds."
Psalm 77:11-12

I feel like it all boils down to God Is Love. He is love in every form. He's the kindest, most loving, perfect parent. That's it in a nutshell. Nothing else matters once you accept Him. I know, as a mom, there's absolutely nothing that could keep me from rescuing my girls or fighting for my girls, or trying everything in my power to do what's best for them. I am by far not a perfect parent. I haven't been consistent in my parenting. It takes so much effort, and some days, I just don't have the energy. And girls are drama! There's always something around here on Days of Our Lives. But God is the perfect parent. He never runs out of energy, He never gives us inconsistent advice, He never fails us, period, and His kids are still messed up and need therapy sometimes. Not because of anything He's done but because we are flawed and we don't listen to Him. I'm always telling the girls, "If you would just listen to me!" I can't imagine how frustrated God gets with us (me).

My devotional today says to remember. Remember all the times God has delivered us from troubles, all the times He's comforted us, all the times we couldn't see a way out of it, and He opened a path. I'm so glad I have this journal. My only regret is that I haven't journaled all the years before when God showed up in my life. Next week is my 2nd treatment, and I will remember how He was with me. I will remember all the blessings from the last 78 days, and I'll remember I am highly favored.

\

Day 84

*Do not conform to the pattern of this world, but be
transformed by the renewing of your mind. Then you will
be able to test and approve what God's will is-his good,
pleasing and perfect will.*
Romans 12:2

My friend Rachel sent me a book called 'Don't Waste Your Cancer.' It is filled with so much great scripture. It helped me see things from another perspective. I've always thought nothing bad or evil can come from God. And it can't really. But He will allow things to happen in our life with a purpose in mind. God could have healed me from cancer before any doctor ever detected it, but He has allowed it in my life with a purpose. I totally believe this. The book looks at cancer as a blessing, a momentary affliction preparing us for eternal glory. This cancer is a witness to God's glory and I cannot waste it.

I have an opportunity that some people may never get and that's to grow closer to Him. It's like a veil has been lifted on another level of my faith, and if I went back to before my diagnosis, I wouldn't have this. I'd rather have this. So, I see what the author means about not wasting it. God knew I would have cancer, and His plan is for me to use it; I'm just not sure how yet. I wish He would reveal His plan to me in a burning bush or a cloud like he did with Moses. Maybe not the burning bush because Chad would have a fit. A billboard would be nice. I'm waiting to see what He wants me to do with all of this. Maybe it's just to encourage myself and some friends along the way. And that's fine with me because my faith is stronger than ever, and I am eternally grateful.

Day 85

"A wife of noble character who can find? She is worth far more than rubies. Her husband has full confidence in her and lacks nothing of value. She brings him good, not harm, all the days of her life."
Proverbs 31:10-12

On our way to chemo number two, I am a tiny bit anxious but mostly hopeful. This is the halfway mark. Only two more treatments after today. This time, Chad is participating in the cold therapy with me. Last time he lovingly told me to "suck it up and do it" because it's better than living with neuropathy. And I agree, but it's torture sitting on ice for 3 hours. So today, I'll be asking the nurse to prepare six ice baths instead of four. And since I am such a wonderful wife, I'm not asking him to do his feet, just hands. Speaking of being a wonderful wife, I thought it would be a good idea for him to schedule some of the things he thinks we need done around the house. Today, we are having some trees taken down. That will help me feel so much better knowing that's all taken care of (said no woman ever). I'll be able to rest and recover tomorrow, listening to the gentle hum of the chainsaws. I'm not wasting this cancer! With all this time off, we have to check off all the honey-dos.

The waiting room is full today. I look like a veteran now; I'm seasoned. A survivor started a conversation with me and asked how many treatments I've had and how soon I lost my hair. She looks amazing! She had eight treatments and finished last June. It was great to see her doing so well. I watch others interacting, and I eavesdrop on their stories. One couple comes bounding up the stairs. We're on the fifth floor. Good for you lady, no trophies here. The elevators are working just fine. I'm getting agitated the longer I sit here. Sometimes, I still feel like I'm watching a TV show, like this isn't my life, but now I look the part. I don't look out of place like I feel I did when I had my long locks. Everyone knows why you're here when you're bald.

Just finished the first bag of chemo. And I ripped those stupid ice bags off as soon as I could. I get in the foulest mood from wearing those things. I HATE it. I'm so sick of the nurse and Chad saying, "It's only 30 more minutes; it's only 20 more minutes." "Well, you wear it then." Ughhhhhhh, I'm so mad. Chad wore ice on one hand. And his hand is so massive it melted the ice in minutes. And his other hand got to TikTok the whole 3 hours, so it doesn't count. I did get to doze off a little bit, which helps pass the time, and my nurse is very kind. They served me lunch, and I picked the chicken Caesar wrap again; it's delicious. I've gained almost 10lbs back from my 42 down. That makes me sad. They say it's the steroids, and they're glad I have an appetite, but they don't know how far I've come, and I don't want to go backwards. Oreos! I just noticed my wrap came with 4 Oreos. BeRightBack.

And while I'm in a foul mood, my NP went over my MRI results. Everything looks good, but they did see a spot on my spleen about a cm. The radiologist is pretty sure it's benign, but they're going to watch it and scan me again in 6 months. She reiterated that he (the radiologist) wasn't too concerned about it. At this point, I don't even know what I'm doing anymore. I'm just here. Floating in and out of my body. I don't know whether to laugh or cry sometimes. I know when I get home and have dinner with my family, I'll feel better, but right now, I can't even stand myself. I could never let a friend bring me to chemo. They couldn't handle this mood. They've all seen it anyway, but I bet if you ask them to sign up for happy Katie or pissy Katie, they would choose option one. The NP also wanted to see how my boils were healing. She seemed perplexed also and asked if I had done any gardening. Hahahahaha, she's a comedian on the weekends, I bet. Lady, if it's above 70°, I am not going outside unless it's to the beach!

Just completed half of my chemo treatments! Still in a bad mood. I'll blame it on the meds. One of them does cause extreme irritability. I have moments every now and then where I can't stand to hear anyone breathe. And I'm still mad at that couple who thought they need-ed to climb five flights of stairs. Rude. I'll come back later if I'm better.

Home isn't better. I swear I think my kids don't even know what I'm going through. It could be several things. Regular teenager stuff, maybe they do realize what I'm going through and can't handle it. I'm thinking it's a combo. But whatever, it is so disheartening to come home to this. I think I really have handled this well in front of them. And behind the scenes, I feel like I'm the same way 90% of the time. I really am not emotional about it. So maybe, in some way, they don't see me upset and think it's no big deal. Or maybe it is a huge deal, but they just don't know how to express it. But all I know is that whatev-er it is, it is very hurtful to me. I've tried to talk to them about how they're feeling, and I've been honest about everything on my end. God knows whatever it is, so I will give Him today and move on.

Day 86

"Create in me a pure heart, O God, and renew a steadfast spirit within me. Do not cast me from your presence or take your Holy Spirit from me. Restore to me the joy of your salvation and grant me a willing spirit, to sustain me. Then I will teach transgressors your ways, so that sinners will turn back to you."
Psalms 51:10-13

Since I was so foul yesterday, I figured this morning was a good time to reflect on the pros I've experienced so far in my journey. Firstly, my relationship with Christ has BOOMED! ✓ ✓ ✓

Secondly, I know how very much I am loved by my friends and family.

Next, No. More. Chin hair. That in itself is a pure miracle. I know it'll probably grow back, but not now! I don't have to shave my legs or armpits. I don't have a period right now, and that may or may not come back; I have not had to cook in months. I'm sure there are things I'm forgetting, too. I don't feel sick or have pain this morning, so that's a relief, but I'm kind of waiting for it to come. Like I'm walking on eggshells, just waiting to turn the corner. It's afternoon and I was able to have a few visitors. I'm pretty tired now, but nothing abnormal. My throat is scratchy, which is another random side effect. But I feel like I want to rest it and make sure it's just that. I'm also having problems connecting my words to my tongue and I stutter some. It's hard to collect my thoughts sometimes and my memory is crap. I can only imagine what the chemo is up to, destroying brain cells that I barely have to begin with. I'm just so grateful that I don't feel badly yet. I have a patch on my arm that releases the meds that cause bone pain. It will be released tonight at 7pm. With all the preventative meds in place, I pray that I'll continue to feel as good as I do now, even though I'm stopping to take a nap.

I don't feel good. I don't want to do this anymore. It's halfway, not counting radiation, but I don't see how people do this and do even more. I don't like it. I don't like it on a box; I don't like it with a fox, I don't like it, Sam. I am. I want cancer to STOP! This time, I feel like I'm having a gallbladder attack, but I don't have a gallbladder anymore. I'm ready to tap out. I'm a terrible sick person; it's not the sick, it's the discomfort. It puts me right back in that awful state.

Day 87

"After Job had prayed for his friends, the Lord restored his
fortunes and gave him twice as much as he had before.
The Lord blessed the latter part of Job's life more than the
former part. He had fourteen thousand sheep, six thousand
camels, a thousand yoke of oxen and a thousand donkeys.
And he also had seven sons and three daughters. After this,
Job lived a hundred and forty years; he saw his children
and their children to the fourth generation. And so Job
died, an old man and full of years."
Job 42:10, 12-13, 16-17

My taste buds are wrong. I can't even enjoy my coffee. Lots of things taste weird now and to top it off I have a cold with a cough. And with the cough, I have tears running down my legs. Not fun.

But I'm reading the Bible story about Job. I've always known his story since I was a kid, but reading it in different translations helps reveal what a good man Job really was. He was so tormented by the horrible things that happened to him because he didn't know why God was allowing it. I don't think anyone went through as much as Job. He literally lost every single thing, person, possession and then his health. But he never lost faith. When all these obstacles arise, I never considered that turning from God would help matters more. I still never wonder why. Why not? Life is not fair; so poor, undeserving Job was tested, his faith did not waver, and in the end, he was blessed twice as much. I have already been blessed so much through this challenge and I'm excited to see what God has in store for me and my family.

Day 88

*"I will give thanks to you, Lord , with all my heart; I
will tell of all your wonderful deeds. I will be glad and
rejoice in you; I will sing the praises of your name, O
Most High. The Lord reigns forever; he has established his
throne for judgment. He rules the world in righteousness
and judges the peoples with equity. The Lord is a refuge for
the oppressed, a stronghold in times of trouble. Those who
know your name trust in you, for you, Lord,
have never forsaken those who seek you."*
Psalm 9:1-2, 7-10

Not much to document. I've been floating around right outside
my body this week. All this medicine makes me feel so disconnected.
When I had chemo the other day, I wore an Elvis shirt. The nurse
said she loved Elvis, and I told her I had named my son Elvis. That's
how it just flowed out of my mouth, but I don't have a son. I was so
frustrated that the nurse said don't worry, whatever you're trying to
say will come. And it finally did. I have a daughter and I named her
Presley after the King of Rock and Roll.

Things are just weird and I don't always feel like myself. I have a
very hard time concentrating. But overall, I am much better this time
around. The bone pain is controlled and I don't feel like giving up. I
know on these days God is literally carrying me with my extra 10 lbs.
and all. I look back over the day and don't even remember being part
of it. He has sustained me and I know He won't leave me. It makes me
long for the days ahead when this will be behind me.

Morning is best for me. My head is clearer and I'm not as loopy.
By late afternoon, I am out of body, just existing. So I'm grateful that I
wake up early and refreshed and that's when I have some quiet time to
reflect. God is so very present with me during every bit of this journey.
I've heard horror stories along the way, and of course, I've had some

snags. But treatment has come a long way over the years and I could be doing so much worse. The support system I have is unbelievable; I am never without a text, a visitor, a phone call, or a gift. It's so insane to be loved so much. Prayer is the most important thing you can ever do for someone and people act like it's the least they can do for me. I feel the effects of prayer. It's very real and I am proof that God hears our cries.

Day 90

"May these words of my mouth and this meditation of my heart be pleasing in your sight, Lord, my Rock and my Redeemer."
Psalm 19:14

Cancer is lonely. No one gets how you feel. There are the ones who've been through it, of course. But as far as my daily life, they don't get it. Since I'm not whiny or pitiful constantly I am expected to be normal, while I have this inner turmoil at all times. I fight with not feeling well, not feeling myself and feeling rage. It's mentally exhausting. I go from 0-60 from one emotion to another, mostly inwardly. Because if I let it out, they'd lock me away. Sometimes I think that would be nice. To go stay at the hospital until all of this is over, having my needs met and only being social when it suits me. I don't like feeling this way. I know it's wrong and uncomfortable for my family too. But sometimes I just want to scream! I don't want any expectations on me of how I should feel or act. There are support groups I could go to, but that's not what I want. I don't want to sit around and talk about cancer crap. I either want to be normal again or just be understood. I know it's asking a lot of others. They don't know, just like I didn't before now. And honestly, I hope no one I love ever knows what I mean firsthand. I long to be empathized with or justified in my feelings. Journaling this has really helped because when I'm feeling good, I can look back and see that this is such a small span of time. I am very loved and reminded of that daily. And, of course, I only have to open my Bible to be reminded of how blessed I am and what Jesus has done for me. I just have more pity parties than I ever have lately and I didn't even get my period this month! Thank God! Who knows what I'd do if that were in the mix?

Day 92

"The Lord makes firm the steps of the one who delights in him; though he may stumble, he will not fall, for the Lord upholds him with his hand."
Psalm 37:23-24

I literally look like Uncle Fester from Addams Family. White bald head, dark circles under my eyes and a rotund belly that is never satiated. I'm eating around the clock, thinking it will make me feel better. All of my meds have to be taken with food. Never a problem. My cold is much better today, but the neuropathy in my fingers is starting. It feels like my hands are asleep, no pain, just annoying. My throat, neck and gums are very tight and tender also. But I am back inside my body today, more myself.

It hasn't been the best day as far as I had planned. Sometimes, we have the best intentions when we start our day, and then somehow, it derails. I let things get right between me and Jesus. It's so easy when things are going how I planned, but the second the train goes off the tracks so do I. I keep going back to "no one understands," but that's not an excuse. I have so much farther to go and I've got to figure out how to keep it together a little better.

So me and Sponge Blob (yes, he's still hanging around) will live to see another day. I'll go to bed early (mainly so I'll stop eating) and get a fresh start tomorrow.

Day 93

*"The Lord detests differing weights,
and dishonest scales do not please him."*
Proverbs 20:23

Who in the history of chemo gains 20 lbs. in two weeks? That would be me. I am destined to be fat. If chemo doesn't make you lose weight, nothing will. Half of the progress I made since last June is gone. I sit here just dumbfounded. I know what I've been shoveling in my mouth, but 20lbs? How many burdens am I carrying? I knew the Uncle Fester resemblance was too close for comfort. One of the bright spots after diagnosis was the probability of losing weight. Everyone in chemo does. Well, not me, apparently. I don't think He trusts me to be a thinner version of myself. I promised I wouldn't dance on the bar (only because I can't climb with this hip). He has to know that! At this point, it's just the cherry on the cake. I will talk to the doctor about it at my appointment this morning. I know what they'll say: oh, it's the steroids, or Oh, we're so glad you have an appetite, or We'll worry about your weight when treatment is over.

Day 96

*"I am not saying this because I am in need, for I have
learned to be content whatever the circumstances. I know
what it is to be in need, and I know what it is to have
plenty. I have learned the secret of being content in any and
every situation, whether well fed or hungry,
whether living in plenty or in want."*
Philippians 4:11-12

I've heard it said that when you can't feel God, that's when He's the closest. I'm sure that's true. He's always with me. He's being very quiet all of a sudden. I'm still seeking out whatever He has in store for me in this journey, but I've grown very weary. And my brain isn't cooperating. I can read and retain what I read, but conversationally, I have a hard time collecting my thoughts and getting them out. I have so many weird things going on with my body collectively that make me not feel good.

It irks me when people say I'm halfway through treatment or there are only 2 more treatments to go. I know they mean well; no one knows the right thing to say, but it's not that. I'm sick and tired of being sick and tired of having this thing to deal with. And God has given me nothing these last few days. I think He wants me to pull up my bootstraps and dig in deep. I'm just so tired. I'm so used to being fed something every day for the last 90 days, and now it's crickets.

Day 97

"One of the servants answered, 'I have seen a son of Jesse of Bethlehem who knows how to play the lyre. He is a brave man and a warrior. He speaks well and is a fine-looking man. And the Lord is with him.'"
1 Samuel 16:18

I feel like cancer is this huge giant in my life. And I am little ol' David fighting the giant Goliath (cancer) with my slingshot of faith. I had told my friend Signe that I felt like God was being silent and she brought me a study book about the life of David. It is so amazing! Reading the Bible alone doesn't give you the full picture of his life, but thankfully, there are theologians who study deeper and explain his life in detail. I've already learned so much about why David was considered a man after God's own heart. He was anointed to be King at such a young age but still continued to tend his father's sheep. I had always assumed once he was anointed, he went straight to being a king. He even slayed Goliath and still had to endure all the mistreatment from King Saul before he would eventually reign. For 40 days, Goliath had taunted the Israeli army. No one would take him on. But on the 41st day, David unknowingly came to check on his brothers and decided to take out Goliath. He had no idea that the forty days prior, Goliath had boasted that he would not be defeated. Goliath mocked God and that infuriated David. David had the confidence of the Lord and obeyed Him. He wasn't weighed down by the last 40 days of the threat.

I have been weighed down by the last 90 days of this giant in my life. I have grown in faith and also struggled with what lies ahead. I want to face this giant with a fresh start. God knows how big and threatening my giant is. It doesn't matter that it's taunted me for 97 days. It's already been defeated and I need to start acting like it. I have zero doubts in Christ. I will start fresh in my obedience and look at this giant as David did on day 41.

Day 98

*"Praise be to the Lord , for he has heard my cry for mercy.
The Lord is my strength and my shield; my heart trusts in
him, and he helps me. My heart leaps for joy, and with my
song I praise him. The Lord is the strength of his people, a
fortress of salvation for his anointed one."*
Psalm 28:6-8

ref·uge: noun - a condition of being safe or sheltered from pursuit, danger, or trouble

Cancer makes me feel like I want to curl up somewhere safe and forget about it for a while. Take refuge, just like when David was running from King Saul and he needed a refuge. He had hit rock bottom, just like I'm feeling now. This is where when you read his psalms, they get really raw and I guess that's me too. He was at the lowest point in his life, and God provided refuge in a cave, and that's when David's life began to turn around. At rock bottom, the only place to look is up. I'm there, too. From there, God was able to prepare David to be king. I'm not sure what God is preparing me for, but He brings comfort in all of life's challenges and in Him, I remember we can be rejuvenated.

Day 99

"I waited patiently for the Lord; he turned to me and heard my cry. He lifted me out of the slimy pit, out of the mud and mire; he set my feet on a rock and gave me a firm place to stand. He put a new song in my mouth, a hymn of praise to our God. Many will see and fear the Lord and put their trust in him. Blessed is the one who trusts in the Lord, who does not look to the proud, to those who turn aside to false Gods. Many, Lord my God, are the wonders you have done, the things you planned for us. None can compare with you; were I to speak and tell of your deeds, they would be too many to declare. Sacrifice and offering you did not desire— but my ears you have opened— burnt offerings and sin offerings you did not require. Then I said, "Here I am, I have come— it is written about me in the scroll. I desire to do your will, my God; your law is within my heart." I proclaim your saving acts in the great assembly; I do not seal my lips, Lord, as you know. I do not hide your righteousness in my heart; I speak of your faithfulness and your saving help. I do not conceal your love and your faithfulness from the great assembly. Do not withhold your mercy from me, Lord; may your love and faithfulness always protect me. For troubles without number surround me; my sins have overtaken me, and I cannot see. They are more than the hairs of my head, and my heart fails within me. Be pleased to save me, Lord; come quickly, Lord, to help me. May all who want to take my life be put to shame and confusion; may all who desire my ruin be turned back in disgrace. May those who say to me, "Aha! Aha!" be appalled at their own shame. But may all who seek you rejoice and be glad in you; may those who long for your saving help always say, "The Lord is great!" But as for me, I am poor and needy; may the Lord think of me. You are my help and my deliverer; you are my God, do not delay"
Psalm 40:1-17

This psalm resonates with me today.

On day 50, I was given Psalm 40. I didn't know at the time that it was the first psalm David wrote after 16 months of running from God. A man after God's own heart had turned away from Him and lived a life of his own. After hitting rock bottom, he finally turned to the only one who could rescue him. Knowing how low David was, God was still there the whole time, waiting for David to surrender.

Day 104

"Be still before the Lord and wait patiently for him; do not fret when people succeed in their ways, when they carry out their wicked schemes."
Psalm 37:7

After days of quietness from God, I feel like I know what He wants me to do now. I'm supposed to wait on Him. I'm supposed to rest and appreciate this period in time and not try to get to the next thing. I am actively waiting on God to show me the next step in my journey because we don't know His timing, and the next step in my journey either isn't ready for me or I am not ready for it.

I can dwell in this quiet time from God and know He's still working and in control and I don't have to do anything but wait. It's very hard for me to be patient or quiet, so this will be a challenge. But I know it's necessary to have this time to grow. I'm always ready for the next step and always need a plan to keep the ball rolling right through to the end of this battle. But God wants me to slow down and actually learn something that I will keep with me even when this battle is over.

Day 105

"Children, obey your parents in everything,
for this pleases the Lord."
Colossians 3:20

On a different note, why is parenting so hard? I can't catch a break. The easiest part of motherhood is squeezing the little things out of your nether regions.

After that, it's the biggest roller coaster you could ever imagine, with harsh, sharp turns, downward spirals and climbs that make your stomach flip. There is no stopping in sight; you can never get off, and only sometimes does it slow down. I love my girls more than anything, and I love being their mom, but some days are so much tougher than others.

Day 108

"For everything that was written in the past was written to teach us, so that through the endurance taught in the Scriptures and the encouragement they provide we might have hope."
Romans 15:4

The nurse who did my IV yesterday for chemo number three taught me everything she's ever known about being a nurse. Geez, lady, I just want to get upstairs and get my chemo over with. But now I'm a certified RN on top of the MD I earned through Grey's Anatomy. I also am a DVM and can deliver a calf thanks to watching the Incredible Dr Pol on Animal Planet. All joking aside, these jobs look so easy at times because the people who do them studied for years and continue to study their practice. The more they practice, the easier it becomes. In my walk through this journey, it's becoming easier and easier to follow God's direction and feel His peace in my life because I'm studying Him more.

Day 109

"For we are God's handiwork, created in Christ Jesus to do good works, which God prepared in advance for us to do.
Ephesians 2:10

"Sometimes God's preparation comes packaged as pain"- Pastor Craig Groeschel

Instead of me asking God what the purpose of all of this is, I have learned that He wants me to get to know Him deeper through this process. If He reveals His plan for my life now, that's all I would focus on instead of learning and growing in my faith. This waiting period is for me to trust wholeheartedly and hear God's voice clearly before He can trust me with whatever He plans to do through this journey. I think if God had revealed to David that He would one day kill a giant, David would have been obsessed with his mission rather than focusing on God. He doesn't need to reveal His will for our lives. We just need to trust the process. As an avid planner this can be very hard for me at times because I'm so desperate to know what's next. I am slowly becoming more trustworthy and letting things happen. He has never failed me, so I'm not sure why I have such a problem with control. But it seems to be easing. I am not worried as much about how and when I'll return to work. I know God will align it perfectly, better than if I took control myself. I struggle with clients depending on me and I am still not dependable as far as how I'm feeling and on what day I will be feeling good enough to work. I know it will work out as it should, so I have to let that go and pray that I won't get overwhelmed as I slowly get back to the salon to work.

Day 110

*"All this is for your benefit, so that the grace that is reaching
more and more people may cause thanksgiving to overflow
to the glory of God. Therefore we do not lose heart.
Though outwardly we are wasting away, yet inwardly
we are being renewed day by day. For our light and
momentary troubles are achieving for us an eternal glory
that far outweighs them all.*
2 Corinthians 4:15-17

I hate to admit this to myself, much less to others who may read this. But in hindsight, I feel like I was very lukewarm in my faith until this diagnosis. My faith has always been solid and I think that's why it's so easy to be lukewarm. I felt I had a safety net. But that's not what faith is. I was taught the devil has us exactly where he wants us when we are not doing anything for the sake of Christ, not telling others about Him. Evil can't have my soul, but it can distract me from sharing God's love and miracles in my life. I know this trial was brought to nudge me in my walk with Christ, and I am grateful for it, as weird as it sounds. It's so hard to see with all of life's distractions, so when something like this comes, it can clear our vision and lift the veil. For so long, I've gone through the motions of life, work, and motherhood. I believe our purpose is so much greater. At the end of the day, I'm so thankful for my firm foundation, and I hope that in any future trials that I might face, I can stand strong. It's hard to know what would cause you to break. I've seen people survive what would be the unsurvivable to me. But we can never know what God has prepared for us and the strength others have shown is an encouragement to me to keep going with my small struggle when their struggle seems so much bigger. I believe struggles show the spirit of God moving in your life.

Day 111

*"Always giving thanks to God the Father for everything, in
the name of our Lord Jesus Christ."*
Ephesians 5:20

Yesterday, I was able to give comfort to a friend whose mom is two months behind me in her breast cancer journey. Her mother lives in Spain and she feels so hopeless to help her from so far away. She said that the information I gave her and the fact that I was doing so well helped to ease her worry. Cancer treatment has really come a long way, even in recent years, especially in the weight gain department. I hate the weight, but I am so grateful not to be sick all the time. And while I wouldn't wish this diagnosis on anyone, overall, it hasn't been as bad as what some people endure. The pain I'm having today is in my neck and jaw. The easiest way to describe it is strep throat. It doesn't hurt to swallow, but all the muscles that are connected to your tongue feel strained. Not much seems to help. I've had it on and off, but today is pretty bad. It feels like your jaw muscles are so tight, but they aren't. And good news, I'm down seven pounds from the 22 I had gained from the steroids. Hopefully, this week, I can, at the least, not gain. I got my period, too, so that's fun. Most patients are in menopause and don't often deal with their period while on treatment. I skipped one, and that was nice. It just adds a level of ugh to deal with. I guess my body is still trying to do what it's supposed to do in spite of the poison coursing through my veins. Today, I cleaned the house, grocery-shopped and cooked dinner. I am very tired, but not too bad. It feels good to get some normalcy back. I even baked a cake, but it wasn't done enough in the middle, but I'm sure it won't go to waste.

Day 114

"The Lord is close to the brokenhearted and saves those who are crushed in spirit."
Psalm 34:18

Today was bearable. As the day progressed, I either got used to feeling like crap, or it was somewhat better. I got a few things checked off of my list and stayed on top of my meds so the pain didn't take over. I'm sure tomorrow will be a lot better. My friends are constantly bringing me things to help, cream for pain, and that seems to help a lot. One of my girlfriends, who is finally done with all of her breast cancer treatment, brought us dinner tonight. It was delicious and seeing her doing so well was most comforting. I can't wait to be on the other side of this and be the one blessing others. I'm not saying I'll cook, but I have so much to give back.

Day 115

Neither height nor depth, nor anything else in all creation,
will be able to separate us from the love of God that is in
Christ Jesus our Lord.
Romans 8:39

I told myself I'd work on my shopping addiction, but today is not that day. With Easter and Harper's birthday coming I was feeling good enough to get some shopping done. The pain has lessened to a dull ache, and if I stay on top of my meds, I can almost ignore it. That's what I love about shopping. It's such a distraction from reality. I focus on the hunt and almost forget my worries. I forget that I'm bald or that I have a huge steroid belly, at least until I try on something in the fitting room. I had a lot of energy and it felt good to get out for a while. Tomorrow, I will do a few clients to get back into some kind of routine, and hopefully, that will keep me from shopping so much.

It took me anywhere between three and five minutes to remember what year it was. I needed a specific date for something, and I could not remember if we were just getting into '22 or '23. My brain was completely blank, and it was kinda scary. I started to wonder if I was losing it. I never did figure it out on my own. I opened the calendar app on my phone, and at the top, it gave me the answer. Chad thinks it's because I haven't been working and using a calendar, but it's not that; I genuinely could not even guess. I can't wait to have this fog lifted.

Day 120

"Why, my soul, are you downcast? Why so disturbed within me? Put your hope in God, for I will yet praise him, my Savior and my God."
Psalm 42:11

The days are blurring together. On those days when I was hurting, I don't remember much; I just went through the motions. Once I'm feeling a little better, I have to play catch-up, and it makes time fly.

Yesterday Pastor spoke on discouragement. Here are the reasons why we don't have to be discouraged. God loves me. Be authentic. Be exactly who God created me to be. Don't pretend. It's ok to feel discouraged sometimes. It's not all about me. The world doesn't revolve around me and my problems. Relax in who He created me to be. Don't fake your feelings. I can use my pain to help others. It's so easy to get discouraged when I focus on my pain. I have a prayer list a mile long that includes others with far worse circumstances than me. When I pray for their needs to be met it makes my problems seem so small. It's ok to be discouraged or depressed sometimes because when I am weak, He is strong, and in my weakness His glory can shine brighter.

Day 121

"I will praise you, Lord , with all my heart; before the
"Gods" I will sing your praise. I will bow down toward
your holy temple and will praise your name for your
unfailing love and your faithfulness, for you have so exalted
your solemn decree that it surpasses your fame. When I
called, you answered me; you greatly emboldened me. May
all the kings of the earth praise you, Lord , when they hear
what you have decreed. May they sing of the ways of the
Lord , for the glory of the Lord is great. Though the Lord is
exalted, he looks kindly on the lowly; though lofty, he sees
them from afar. Though I walk in the midst of trouble,
you preserve my life. You stretch out your hand against the
anger of my foes; with your right hand you save me. The
Lord will vindicate me; your love, Lord , endures forever—
do not abandon the works of your hands."
Psalm 138:1-8

Just as I'm starting to feel good, it's time for my last chemo. I hope this is the last push to make sure every cancer cell is dead. Until then, I will try to soak up every ounce of feeling good. I'm really hopeful that I can get through the day tomorrow without being too tired. I have a few friends coming to visit again, and it always fills my cup to listen and talk about other people's interests, and we solve the world's problems together.

Presley was invited to prom with a girlfriend who is a senior, and we will spend the weekend getting them ready for the dance. On another note, our kitten Olive is in heat. I've never experienced this because I've always had my animals neutered before it happened; poor thing is miserable. I was hoping to get through all of my crap before I had to have her fixed. The soonest I could have her scheduled is the end of April. So now we have 4 hormonal females in the house and it is not fun.

Day 125

*"Your beauty should not come from outward adornment,
such as elaborate hairstyles and the wearing of gold jewelry
or fine clothes."*

Imagine being so hideous that your face ID on your phone doesn't recognize you. I got lots of looks last night as I was walking into the store before I realized I didn't have my hat on. I rushed back to the car to get it. I must have looked like a meet and greet for Uncle Fester from the Adams Family at Comicon. It's going to be ages before I have any semblance of a hairstyle. If I wasn't gaining weight also, I'd be ok with it. But I'm still eating around the clock. Food and shopping have always been such a comfort, even more so now. I know it's better than being sick, but I will be so mad at myself when this is over to have to lose this weight again.

Day 126

"Carry each other's burdens, and in this way you will fulfill the law of Christ."

Tomorrow, I will complete my chemo treatments and then begin the process of preparing for radiation. Life will pile things up rather than give us one thing at a time to deal with. So, just because I have this going on does not mean I can put this struggle (parenting a preteen) on the back burner. I will be committed to improving my parenting while finishing this fight for my health. I've been so emotional today. I think in the back of my mind, I'm anxious about my last chemo. I know that I won't be feeling good and I don't want to do it. I'm also carrying the weight of the world on my shoulders literally. I know I shouldn't. But the state of our world weighs so heavily on me. I like to be up to date on current events, and the collapse of our society, in general, has me upset.

I'm usually so good at laying my cares at His feet, but not today for some reason. I could list a string of circumstances that have pained me, but it doesn't matter. Everyone gets bombarded with daily trials, and thankfully, His mercies are new. Even though I'll be sitting in that awful place with my hands in ice!! Ugh! I hate it so much. I'll be so glad to ring that bell.

Day 127

*"'They will fight against you but will not overcome you, for
I am with you and will rescue you,' declares the Lord."*
Jeremiah 1:19

Today, I am done with chemo. That is all. I am so thrilled to have this portion of my journey behind me. I had no idea how emotional it would be to physically ring that bell now that I know the meaning behind it. I feel so honored to have been able to ring it and signify the end of this chapter in my life.

Day 129

"And we know that in all things God works for the good of those who love him, who have been called according to his purpose."
Romans 8:28

I did not sleep last night. Steroids make me so restless. I feel awful, and I know as the day continues, I'll feel worse. So, I got up early to run the last few errands I had before the Easter craziness began. I'm hoping to make it to church Sunday and I'd like a pink hat to wear with my dress. So I said a small prayer that I'd find a hat in the perfect shade of pink right when I walk into the first store. So what happened? Naturally, as #Godsfave, I walked in and directly to my right, hanging on the wall, is the pink hat in the very shade I had envisioned wearing. So I grabbed it and checked out! Thank God for the little things! I still had so many errands to run and that one should've taken the longest. By the time I was done, I was exhausted. The rest of the day was a blur; just trying to hang on and engage in the moment. The kids had a lot going on with friends and activities that I needed to interact with, but I can't remember much.

Two nights ago, we were able to take the kid's ax-throwing; my nephew came down from Georgia. It was really fun! I did not participate for fear of popping another boob. I don't want two Sponge Blobs to deal with. Besides, I had no strength to throw an ax after having chemo the day before. Me and Epsom had our time together and I loaded up on sleep meds. Looking forward to actual rest.

Day 130

"What, then, shall we say in response to these things? If God is for us, who can be against us? He who did not spare his own Son, but gave him up for us all—how will he not also, along with him, graciously give us all things?"

Days have gone by in a blur, including Easter. I made it to church and was so grateful, but that was it. I slept pretty much ever since until today. Thank God I never have to have another chemo, it sucks. I can't even gather my thoughts enough to write or reflect. I love to read and I'm not really able to when I'm like this. I'm so glad that part of the journey is behind me and I can focus on getting back to normal

We watched the Passion of the Christ for the first time as a family Saturday night as well, and I couldn't let myself go there. It's too overwhelming to reflect on all He's done for me and what He went through on that first Easter. I think I have disconnected myself emotionally from these things while I'm not feeling great because it takes more energy than I have right now. I remember the first time I watched The Passion and how overcome I was by the reality of it all, and now watching it as a mother myself is just too much

I made a roast in the crock pot for Easter dinner, and the girls loved their Easter baskets, and I loved my Oxy and bed. Chad has hurt his knee somehow, so we are a real pair. We are a sight for sore eyes as we hobble and wobble around with our disabilities. Harper just rolls her eyes and says, "Ugh! Y'all are so old!"

So, I have no encouragement to give myself or others right now because I don't have the energy. I know He is here with me and that's enough.

Day 137

Wait for the Lord; be strong and take heart and wait for the Lord.
Psalms 27:14

Church today was just what I needed. I was about to crack. My family didn't want to go to church with me this morning, and the whole drive there alone made me feel like such a failure when it came to my family. We've had one struggle after another, and I am the parent; I should have all the solutions, right? I'm also a naturally happy person who hasn't been feeling very happy lately. After reading all about David and his struggles and triumphs, I couldn't decide which character to study next. This morning God made it clear that Paul is the one I should study. I had no idea he wrote so many books of the Bible and all with a happy perspective from prison!

This morning, I was so discouraged by many things. When the paths we are on suddenly end, it leaves us feeling like we failed or we are lost. But we are not. Paul's life goal was to preach at the Roman Coliseum. He wanted to reach as many for Christ as possible. Instead, he was imprisoned. That was not his plan at all, but it did not discourage him. During his imprisonment he was able to witness over 4,000 Roman guards. Their families came to Christ right under the authority of Caesar, who imprisoned Him. How many more know Christ because of the influence Roman soldiers must've had? I was encouraged today because I was reminded that even if we sway from God's will or make mistakes along the way, He can still make it work for his glory. So right now, when things look messy and I don't have a plan, I can feel confident in His plan for me and my family. And even when I don't know what else to do, I believe He has it all under control.

Because seriously, we jump on airplanes without ever meeting the pilot and trust him completely to get us to our destination. I should be able to trust in our Heavenly Father to help me arrive safely in my life's journey.

Day 140

*"See, I am doing a new thing! Now it springs up; do you
not perceive it? I am making a way in the wilderness and
streams in the wasteland."*
Isaiah 43:19

I got my first tattoo today- three actually! Tiny little dots to help
pinpoint the accuracy of my radiation. But that will not be the complete end to this journey; I'll still need Sponge Blob repaired. But
yay me! I can't wait for this to be over with. I'm so tired from my
appointment today and the long drive. I had my CT simulation and
it was crazy. Laser beams point in every direction like some Mission
Impossible movie, but I am far from being Tom Cruise. Besides, he
has more hair than me.

I laid in a bed of what felt like moon sand or the moon dough
that my kids used to play with. Naked above the waist, with my arms
above my head, freezing, they began to shape the dough around my
head, arms and torso. Into the tube, I went while horrible renditions
of oldies played on Muzak. I'd much rather be cold than have a drop
of sweat, so it wasn't unbearable. My whole team was all men and
one woman; she was in charge, of course. I just laid back and closed
my eyes while they worked expertly. Once the mold was done, the
scan began. Sometimes, I had to hold my breath. The radiologist will
decide if I need to hold my breath for treatment or not. Something
about air in my lungs makes more room between my heart and the
radiation space. For a chubby girl, holding your breath is not so easy.
And Sponge Blob did not behave; he fell under my armpit, and I'm
just over him.

The radiology techs were all around me, lifting Sponge Blob
and tucking the moon dough into me; it was almost relaxing. Then,
the marking started. I smelled the marker before I felt it. Cold and
smooth on my skin, almost ticklish. They're very efficient as they work

and try to be as discreet as they can without a boob sneaking out if they can help it. One of the techs and I discovered we grew up in the same town. And our kids are friends at school! And now he's seen me naked. Great. Bet he's never seen the odd pair I've got! I bet he goes home to his daughter and says, "Don't ask for a playdate with Harper. I've seen her mother naked.

Day 142

*"So that through my being with you again your boasting in
Christ Jesus will abound on account of me."*
Philippians 1:25

It feels so good to have real and meaningful conversations with my clients again. I realized today that I hug each of my clients and tell them I love them because I really do! I have missed these relationships so much; each person brings something different to our friendship. I love talking about their lives and laughing. Of course, I talk about myself a lot more these days, and I spill any and every detail they can handle, with pictures, too, if they have the stomach for it. I was tired by the end of the day (1/2 day) but a good tired. My cup was full, kind-of-tired. And I have my own money in my pocket!

I like having my own and not having to feel like I shouldn't indulge. Chad's a good manager of money. I am not. I am a "spend it like it's the last day of your life" person. I pay my bills, of course. And I've never not been able to pay bills by the grace of God. But if it were up to me, we'd be living under an overpass somewhere dressed in the finest attire, of course. So, in a way, we balance each other. He's currently wearing a pair of shorts that are 17 years old. Obviously, they are stretchy. I can still fit in my earrings from high school. He spends money thinking of our future and I spend money thinking of today. God always provides, even though I could be more disciplined. The reality of my diagnosis kind of made my habit worse. Because you really never know when your last day could come. I am fortunate enough not to have a terminal illness, but there are many who do, and you just can't take it (money) with you. My goal after this is behind me is to have better money management and take better care of myself. But I will never take for granted another day. I am so blessed to celebrate life, even though it's not always easy.

Day 143

"Do not be deceived: God cannot be mocked. A man reaps what he sows. Whoever sows to please their flesh, from the flesh will reap destruction; whoever sows to please the Spirit, from the Spirit will reap eternal life. Let us not become weary in doing good, for at the proper time we will reap a harvest if we do not give up."
Galatians 6:7-9

This morning, I needed a little nap. As I drifted off to sleep, I was startled awake by the most dreaded sound every pet owner hates to hear. I jumped up faster than lightning as Theo was puking on the rug. Why is it always the rug?? All this wood and he goes to the rug?? These are the things that make me ask why. Why can't I take a nap without a catastrophe? Why does the neighbor's rooster crow all day long? Why is it always something? Why did I keep waking myself up snoring? Could it be the 25 pounds I've packed on? If I have to start napping with my CPAP, I'm calling it quits. I am one big fat disaster. I worked three days this week. Not full days, but enough to fill my cup and be exhausted in a good way. I love laughing and talking about everything under the sun. So many different subjects in a matter of an hour. We go from laughing to crying to laughing again. Tonight, we are having dinner with some friends. They're some of the sweetest people I've ever met, and they have taken Presley in as one of their own. Making new friends as an adult is hard, so when you find people with similar values, it's so refreshing. As tired as I am, I'm really looking forward to going out as a couple while the kids have plans of their own.

Day 148

"He will wipe every tear from their eyes. There will be no more death' or mourning or crying or pain, for the old order of things has passed away."
Revelation 21:4

The tears won't stop falling. I'm not sad. I'm mad. Well, I am having a bit of a pity party. I'm grieving my old self. The one I didn't take care of. I want her back and to start over. I'm at my clinic appointment for blood work and to discuss my future medication. It's all just overwhelming. I will never be the same person again. For the next 10 years, I'll be immune-compromised; I have arthritis all over my body. I assume, from 25 years of hairdressing, I'll have lots of bone loss and on and on. I will be taking a chemo pill for 10 years, another pill for 2 years, and a shot in my butt once a month for 5-10 years, all with a variety of side effects that are not pleasant. Basically, shutting down all female hormones. I'll have mood swings, hot flashes, vaginal dryness, skin changes, joint pain. When you vow for better or worse, you don't really know what will come up. If I were Chad, I'd run. Run Forest run. Who could blame him? I have a longer list of ailments than Bubba Gump has shrimp. It's not going to be fun. And all of this to try and ensure I won't have cancer again, but there is no guarantee. Some of the medications can even cause cancer. I'm in a pit that I just can't climb out of. Just when I start to see the light at the end of the tunnel, it goes dark again. I know I'll feel better again soon, but I have to document this feeling now so that when it's over, I will have gratitude. When I feel this way, I just want to give up. Stop everything. I know the feeling will pass. One good luncheon with friends is sure to heal. But I hate the thought of this being part of my life. And just like that, God sends you just what you need when you need it. These people at Moffitt are incredible. They have pumped my head so full I may float away. I guess one of my love languages is words of affirmation because

I got a load of it today and I am feeling so much better. Thank you, Jesus, for being a provider, even in the little things. I got my first shot today. In the butt. It'll be like the flu shot; it goes deep into the muscle (in my case, fat) and will be very sore. Every month for a decade. Out of all the possible side effects in the world, not one of them is weight loss. None of the drugs cause weight loss.

Day 151

*In peace I will lie down and sleep, for you alone, Lord,
make me dwell in safety.*
Psalms 4:8

I would never have to wear a bra again if it weren't for Sponge Blob. I have some thin pullover-type bras that are very comfy. Zero support, but keep Sponge Blob in one place.

Today, I've been so busy. I took our cat Olive to get spayed this morning, came home to do laundry, went back to pick up Olive and came home and started cleaning the house. I got so sweaty, so I went to adjust my bra, and Sponge Blob was completely out of the bra! Good boob in. Bad titty out. And I have no idea how long ago he moved out of his second home because I have zero feeling. I'm still completely numb. So now, when people stare at me, I have no idea if it's because I'm bald or because I have lopsided titties. I can only imagine the scene I must have been earlier. Bald chubby lady, climbing out of Chad's massive tank of a truck, one titty in, one titty out, with a kitty cat under my arm, waddling my way across the street to drop off Olive at the vet's office.

Tomorrow, my baby will be 13. She is so incredible in so many ways. If she could only see herself through my eyes. She has so many gifts and talents, she loves/hates passionately, people would kill for her eyelashes, and her artistic ability is award-winning; I know she is God's perfect creation. He made her just the way she is and He made me her mother for a reason. One day I will look back on these challenges of raising teenagers and be able to see the amazing woman she has become. Through parenting, God is working on me. I'm still not sure what I'm supposed to be learning because I feel like a big fat failure, but I'm in it for the long haul. I love my babies more than they'll ever know. He reminded me of a song I sang as a child

"He's still working on me to make me what I need to be. It took him just a week to make the moon and stars, the sun and the earth and Jupiter and Mars. How loving and patient He must be 'cause He's still workin' on me..."

Day 153

"Answer me when I call to you, my righteous God. Give me relief from my distress; have mercy on me and hear my prayer. Fill my heart with joy when their grain and new wine abound. In peace I will lie down and sleep, for you alone, Lord , make me dwell in safety."
Psalm 4:1, 7-8

The reality of radiation starting tomorrow and the next five weeks is starting to settle in. I'm not scared or worried; just concerned about my stamina of getting up so early and then trying to work. I also have a cold right now, and the realization that I may never have my good immune system back is troubling. I've had a cold twice in the last two months. And for me, that's usually all I get for the year. And when the radiation journey is finished, I will still have the shots and pills for a decade. I've got to take it one day at a time. I can get through the next five weeks, and then, hopefully, it's downhill from there.

Day 154

Rejoice in the Lord always. I will say it again: Rejoice!
Let your gentleness be evident to all. The Lord is near. Do
not be anxious about anything, but in every situation,
by prayer and petition, with thanksgiving, present your
requests to God. And the peace of God, which transcends
all understanding, will guard your hearts and your minds
in Christ Jesus. Finally, brothers and sisters, whatever is
true, whatever is noble, whatever is right, whatever is pure,
whatever is lovely, whatever is admirable—if anything
is excellent or praiseworthy—think about such things.
Whatever you have learned or received or heard from me,
or seen in me—put it into practice.
And the God of peace will be with you.
Philippians 4:4-9

First radiation wasn't radiation. It was a simulation of what radiation will be starting tomorrow. Scan after scan and X-rays to make sure my placement is perfect. The doctor decided I would need to hold my breath on and off for the duration of the treatment. It doesn't seem like it would be a big deal, but it is. The position I have to lay in and the nakedness and the temperature of the room. It's just all so strange. My hands are above my head, holding my wrists, while my head is turned as far to the left as possible, all while laying on a hard slab topless. It's as fun as it sounds. For each picture they took today, I had to inhale and hold anywhere from 5-15 seconds. After several minutes of that, it gets old. Especially after half an hour.

Once the doctor approved everything, I was free to go. My arms were asleep, and I was a little dizzy. The tech tells me to practice holding my breath tonight in preparation for tomorrow's treatment. I asked how long I'd be holding my breath, assuming it would be like today. He said 60 seconds each time. What boy? I'm sorry my ears are a bit stuffy from this cold. Did you say 60 seconds every time? I think it's obvious I'm no athlete, and I'm definitely not a scuba diver. I may survive this cancer only to pass out and die holding my breath for this crap! Holding my breath for a minute one time may be ok but several times over 30 minutes? He said it was ok to breathe, but the radiation would stop every time I took a breath, and we'd have to restart. At this pace, we'll be there all night. How do these old people do it? I guess not everyone has to, but my doctor likes the space it creates between my heart and lungs.

So anyway, the best part of today was when my friends insisted at the last minute to take me to lunch and my appointment, and they showed up wearing shirts that say, 'Cancer touched Katie's boob, so she kicked its ass'. I can't wait to wear mine once I actually do kick this thing once and for all. I wouldn't have made it this far without my friendships. 154 days of true friends. I still get so emotional about the support I receive. Once I kick this thing, I may miss all this attention. I'll have to come up with another way to get it that doesn't involve sickness or hair loss.

Day 155

"Put on the full armor of God, so that you can take your stand against the devil's schemes."
Ephesians 6:11

Real radiation was today. The treatment wasn't bad except for the uncomfortableness of it all: no sounds or lasers, just huge pieces of metal circling around me. I did have to hold my breath, but not for 60 seconds, thank God. I shouldn't be tired yet, but I am barely hanging on at 7pm. I think the shot, combined with treatment this morning, is wearing on me. We'll see how I hold up next week, getting up super early for treatment and then working for a few hours. I'm sure I can do it; I can do hair without even concentrating; it's become second nature, especially since most of my clients have been with me for so long. I just hope they get a good version of me. Right now, I feel like I'm in a fog. This cold could still be playing a part in that, too, even though it's almost gone and my ears have been stuffy for months, but the doctor says they're fine. I can tell I'm rambling, so I think it's time for bed.

Day 156

*"Resist him, standing firm in the faith, because you
know that the family of believers throughout the world is
undergoing the same kind of sufferings."*
1 Peter 5:9

Tired doesn't even begin to explain how I feel about this cancer crap. I'm exhausted physically and mentally. Sometimes I can't even shed a tear or muster a prayer. But God knows my needs and sometimes I just need to go to bed and let Him handle it.

Day 157

"The Lord is good to all; He has compassion on all He has made."
Psalm 145:9

I had the privilege of shaving my fellow cancer friend's head today. It was so rewarding for me to see her strength and support system; it was very fulfilling. She's only 38 and has triple-negative breast cancer. Our journeys overlapped at Moffitt and now we are forever bound by a sisterhood that no one wants to be part of. It was so nice to have someone with the same

feelings and thoughts going through this at the same time. I've had people reach out to me about their past experiences with cancer, but to have someone currently battling with you at

the same time is somehow different. I can see myself in her. I can see it as a big deal but also just as a part of life. I see her strength and I see also that she doesn't have a choice but to be strong. I don't want to waste my cancer; I want it to be for a reason. It is for a reason. The purpose may never be revealed to me, but I will never stop searching for it.

Day 160

"For the Lord is good and his love endures forever; his faithfulness continues through all generations."
Psalm 100:5

Today was ick. I finally went to bed last night, not feeling great. As I struggled to fall asleep, my throat and ears began to ache. I thought I was getting another cold when I barely just got over the last one. The doctor checked my ears last week and they were fine. So that means it's my lymph nodes. The radiation to my lymphatic system includes my neck. Sore throat is one of the many symptoms. So, I turned off my alarm in the middle of the night and decided I would try to sleep in and not go to church. I was able to sleep late for me. Tomorrow starts my early appointments for radiation. I'm ready to see how I do with this schedule. Getting up early and then working and hopefully having the energy to cook dinner and go to bed early. I may end up liking that routine, especially if I can somehow fit walking into the equation. I've got to get on top of this weight gain again. I haven't had steroids in a month now and haven't dropped a pound.

Day 164

"Walk in obedience to all that the Lord your God has commanded you, so that you may live and prosper and prolong your days in the land that you will possess."
Deuteronomy 5:33

I think I'll start referring to radiation as my "spa treatment." I'm only there for a short time every day, but the therapists are so much fun, and everyone is so unbelievably nice. Even at 7am! I lay on this narrow table and stared up at my reflection as they shifted and wiggled me into the perfect position. Looking at myself, I could either cry or pretend it looked like a scene from a sad movie. My hairless head and nippleless breasts staring back at me. A huge machine enclosing all around me making creepy clicking noises. The camera (I have no idea if it's a camera) stares down at me like a huge eye from a mother ship. It feels like some weird sci-fi movie where the aliens use machines to dissect you. The green laser beams crisscross across my chest, and all I can think about is what this is doing to my organs. There's a beautiful mural on the ceiling, but I have to keep my head turned all the way and can hardly see it. I'm sure it's to help distract you from what's really going on. The techs get me settled and then go into a glass room where they talk to me over the speaker, telling me to breathe, hold, breathe again, over and over until it's done. Then they gently cover me up and help me down off the table, and we all say, "See ya tomorrow!" I've even made friends with some of the reception people, and a few old guys who are patients tell me they'll see me tomorrow, too.

Day 165

"For the Lord is good and His love endures forever;
His faithfulness continues through all generations."
Psalm 100:5

What was I thinking? Over here, footloose and fancy-free, living my best life. All the fun and games are over. I pulled out the 10x mirror. The chin hairs are back. How foolish I have been to think they were gone. It's been months since I had to worry about this horrible curse. And where are all my so-called "friends?" No one has said a word! You can clearly see the fuzz on my scalp so I know you can see the black witch hairs on my chin. I can't believe this. I feel like I deserve at least this one thing to end. And now that my ovaries are being murdered, I'm sure my goatee will become even more prominent. I'm not sure who I'd rather look like: Powder from the 1995 movie or Bruce Willis with a goatee. Whatever. I'm going to have to start shaving my legs again, too. It was fun while it lasted.

Day 167

"Children are a gift from the Lord;
they are a reward from him."
Psalm 127:3

Ahhhhh Mother's Day. I joke every year that all I want is to be a dad.

To me, every day is Father's Day. They get to do whatever they want whenever they want. Sure, they have different sets of responsibilities and pressures, but being so unattached is a feeling I'm just starting to remember. Dads can just go to the store, or just mow the lawn—no need for daycare or a sitter. I used to get so mad at the difference in parenting. I've heard stories of moms who didn't shower for days and let themselves go and stopped buying nice underwear. I vowed that wouldn't be me. I never did miss a shower, but I can say my panties have seen better days. My pediatrician said no baby has ever died from crying, so put the baby down and take a shower. I remember one time I did just that: I put Presley in her bouncy seat on the bedroom floor with the TV on baby Einstein while I showered. She began crying about halfway through and I remembered what the doctor said. A little crying wouldn't hurt. When I finished my shower and went into the bedroom, Presley was hanging head-first onto the floor with her little legs still strapped into the bouncy seat, crying. At least I knew enough to sit it on the floor and not the bed or she may not be here today.

It's a miracle any of us make it through.

Of course, I look back and adore the time of raising babies. That was the easy part for me. No discussion about what they will eat or what they will wear, holding them and rocking them. But I remember the times when I could drop everything and go, just like a man. Or when I wasn't thinking about someone else's well-being 24 hours a day. I am still doing that. I suppose that will never end. And I don't want it to because that will mean they're completely self-reliant. And as much as that's natural, and I want that for my girls, it's sad to think they may not need me. It's the natural God-designed way, and then we can be friends, I hope.

And not that dads don't worry or carry emotional bonds with their kids, but I don't know a single one who knows their kid's lunch number, teacher's names or bus numbers. One of my and Chad's biggest fights was about a lunch number. Presley had left her lunch box at home, and I was going to be late for work, so I needed him to drop it at school. I flipped out that he didn't know her student number. The weight of all the little things moms have to know adds up. It's a wonderful weight to have the privilege of carrying, but sometimes, we just want to set it down for a minute. Mother's Day is a day to remind ourselves of that. It's hard because you want to honor your own mother and mother-in-law, but in doing that, you don't get a rest yourself. I have an excuse for this year, of course. Being a mom is the most frustrating and rewarding job in the world. I'd never trade it for a million bucks, maybe ten million. I love my girls and I'm so glad I'm their mom, even though sometimes I'd rather be the dad.

Day 168

And our hope for you is firm, because we know that just as you share in our sufferings, so also you share in our comfort."
2 Corinthians 1:7

Today, I wanted to complain about how long my radiation and doctor's appointments were taking, but I couldn't. As I waited in the comfy chairs of the newly redecorated waiting area, I was approached by three different women at three different times. There's a kind of silent sisterhood I automatically feel. Sometimes, it's just a look out in public when you see a fellow survivor, as if we get each other. Each woman today had a different journey, of course, and I was able to share my faith a little and let them know I would be praying for them. My prayer list includes so many new people I've met on my journey. I try to get everyone's name, but sometimes I just have their description written down with their diagnosis in parentheses; God knows who they are.

I'm fortunate to love all of my doctors and nurses and my prognosis is one of the best ones you can get. Each woman has had a harder journey or a grimmer diagnosis. Days like this let me know there are far greater reasons to be on the path I'm on. I feel so fortunate in a waiting room filled with seemingly hopeless people. My faith is definitely the only reason I'm able to face this. I hope I'm able to meet even more amazing women in the second half of radiation.

Day 170

*Let us not become weary in doing good, for at the right
time we will reap a harvest if we do not give up.*
Galatians 6:9

Today is the halfway mark! 12/25 radiation treatments complete!
It's definitely gone faster than I thought it would. I've made so many
friends at the seven reception desks that as soon as they see me walk
in, they check me in and I don't have to wait in line. All the employees
seem to love their jobs and everyone has a smile and a compliment
to give. I think I may miss starting my day out this way, minus the
treatment, of course.

Day 178

My soul is weary with sorrow;
strengthen me according to your word.
Psalm 119:28

Welp. Just left my plastics appointment. Looks like Sponge Blob may be with me for a very long time. Radiation breaks down the skin and its effects won't fully be seen for weeks after completion. By then, my beloved surgeon will be retired and I will be left in the very capable hands of another. But every doctor practices uniquely. My next doctor may not have the same plan for Sponge Blob that I had envisioned. So, I'll wait another month to see the full outcome of what radiation will do to my body before adopting Sponge Blob into the family completely. I have to remember where I was at the beginning of all of this. I told the doctor I would not care how my breasts looked; I just wanted the cancer gone, and he told me that I would care. He was right; I do care. So, I will not complain about him anymore, but I am not ready to give Sponge Blob our last name just yet.

I heard a very encouraging word today. These words are not mine, but they are every bit as encouraging as what I have experienced in my journey.

The person explained:

"Tragedy offers us the opportunity to encounter the truth of who Jesus is. How would we know healing, if we never know disease? How will we know peace without feelings of depression? How can we feel what it means to be alive without ever facing death? Or life without thoughts of death? How will we know restoration if we never fall apart? We can find the truth of Jesus in the rubble of our lives. And even though we don't want to go through certain things, He meets us there and shows us who He is."

I thought this was so beautiful. Because it's so easy to go through life and be a Christian on the surface, but until you come across any of these things I feel you haven't really experienced what Jesus is all about. I think to live a life without turmoil would be to live without the fullness of God, and I don't want that. I sure don't like turmoil and distress, but I wouldn't trade what I have gained.

Day 184

"Remember this: Whoever sows sparingly will also reap sparingly, and whoever sows generously will also reap generously."
2 Corinthians 9:6

Four more days. My armpit looks like an old leather briefcase. It's so tender and hideous looking. I won't be able to tell the difference between the leather seats in my car and my armpit! Sponge Blob is leathery too. Sponge Blob leather pants. And all this happened overnight, just like they said. I'm in a funk again, too. I hate it when I get like this. I have zero energy to do anything. I have kept my house clean, though; that's for my sanity. I'll be done with this part soon, so I'll wallow a little longer. I hate that we don't have any summer plans and nothing to look forward to, but it's ridiculous to try and plan around all these doctors' appointments.

This morning, another fellow patient rang the bell. We all cried and cheered for him and got to meet his wife. It's so weird the closeness we feel to one another from connecting every morning on our separate journeys. There's a strange comfort in being around others in this terrible position. Still, I am the one with the best prognosis. One of the older men has a glioblastoma tumor on his brain. There were no symptoms except he couldn't find words sometimes when he was talking. By the time they found it, it was huge. They couldn't remove it all, so they're radiating the rest. He and his wife are so sweet and I've enjoyed our chats every morning. Another older man and his wife (all the men bring their wives, and all the women tough it out on their own) have an HPV mass in his neck. His neck looks like my armpit, leather. He also has lost 40 lbs. because of throat discomfort when he eats. I sure haven't had that problem. Right now, I feel like I'm in a holding zone, waiting to be finished with this portion so I can mentally move forward. I'm not depressed, really, just kinda stuck. So, I'm really looking forward to Tuesday when I can close this chapter and hopefully make some plans for the future.

Day 185

"Others, like seed sown on good soil, hear the word, accept it, and produce a crop—some thirty, some sixty, some a hundred times what was sown."
Mark 4:20

Three days left. I can do it. I got out my hairbrush today. I miss the sensation of the bristles on my scalp. A few insanely long red hairs were still in it. I'm not sure what I felt when I saw them. I don't know the girl they belonged to anymore; she's different now. I miss her terribly some days. The new girl's schedule is dominated by doctors and appointments. Her joints hurt all the time. She dreams of the day she can be free to book a vacation.

Anyway, the bristles felt so good on my scalp, and it helps to stimulate growth in the follicle. I still have some shiny spots on my scalp where I'm waiting for my hair to come in. I'm not sure if I'll ever have that long red hair again, but I have gained other things along the way, not just weight. I see life through different lenses. Sometimes, it makes me more patient than I would've been before. And sometimes, it makes me more frustrated than I would've been before. I definitely know who I can count on and who means what they say. I know Jesus has got me, no matter what. I see my faults as a friend, mother and wife. Working on them is another story. I can't say I'm working to get back to the person I used to be. Instead, I'm figuring out who the new girl is and what she's supposed to do with all this.

Day 189

"Have I not commanded you? Be strong and courageous.
Do not be afraid; do not be discouraged, for the Lord your
God will be with you wherever you go."
Joshua 1:9

Sponge Blob is decked out in full leather, head to toe. But guess what? Tomorrow is the last day! Day 190 is the last treatment I will ever have to do. I'm so glad the worst is over. I'm not even sure how to feel about it. I still have dozens of appointments scheduled for the next several months as each team sees me for the last time before I go on a maintenance plan. I'm not sure I can sleep tonight for being so excited this chapter is finally over. God has carried me the entire time. I know I will look back and think how I made it through, but I already know. I couldn't have done it without my faith.

DAY 190

It's OVER!

My treatment journey is complete and I couldn't be happier
The car was decorated with balloons
and we wore matching T-shirts that Dina made.
Mine says "Cancer touched my boob so I kicked its ass".
But I couldn't have done it without my faith and
my incredible support system.

*"Let us hold unswervingly to the hope we profess, for he
who promised is faithful."*
Hebrews 10:23

It's OVER! My treatment journey is complete, and I couldn't be happier. There were a few hiccups in the plan at first; the machine was down again, and they wanted to reschedule me for 5:30pm this evening. But it all worked out. I was able to celebrate with my radiation techs, and my friends made my day so special. The car was decorated with balloons, and we wore matching T-Shirts that Dina had made. Mine says, "Cancer touched my boob, so I kicked its ass." But I couldn't have done it without my faith and my incredible support system. I've never gone a day without someone reaching out to let me know I'm being prayed for and thought of. So many times, I wanted to be done, and now I really am. Six months of my life dedicated to this. Now, I can begin to move forward. I still have some things to sort out: getting my ovaries removed, taking chemo pills, and, of course, re-homing Sponge Blob Leather pants. Those things will come in time. Right now, I can finally relax and reflect on everything God has delivered me from and continue to share that with others.

Day 212

*"Even though I walk through the darkest valley,
I will fear no evil, for you are with me;
your rod and your staff, they comfort me."*

It's harder now, the after. Six months ago, my life was turned upside down. And now I'm...normal? But I'm not. My emotions are a wreck. I don't feel good, hardly at all. And it's so hard for people to understand. It's not their fault for not knowing. And I'm not one to complain much. What good does it do? But I am not the same and I fear I may never be. I know a lot of it is the shots I'm getting to kill my ovaries and my pain is from the chemo pills. Once I have my ovaries out, maybe things will balance out. I am worried about the second chemo pill that I have to take for the next two years. It has many different side effects that have made me wary. I've never had any hesitancy about anything in this whole process until now. Maybe I've had more time to process things. And I'm realizing this is far from over. Clients think I'm done, better, past all of the cancer stuff. And I am healed, but to ensure that it doesn't reoccur, I have so much still to do. It's daunting. The days of me worrying about Sponge Blob are over. I don't even care about him anymore. He's somewhat more stable, so I've put him out of my mind. Now it's on to ovary removal. And taking off work again just when I was starting to catch up. I feel alone and I know I'm not. But my situation is lonely. No two survivors have the same story, but it does help to connect on mostly common ground. I wonder if others have felt this way as well. Cancer is never far from my mind. As much as I don't want it to be part of me, it is. I can't escape it completely. Severe diarrhea is my next focal point. This new medicine that I should've started today causes that without exception. The doctor said it will happen. I am to carry Imodium at all times. This is not convenient for my career. I'm 43 years old. I shouldn't be worrying about this for at least 30 more years. And I know others have it far worse. That's why I've got to get these emotions under control. I need to be grateful it's not worse and grateful God healed me, grateful I can work and grateful that everyone thinks I'm normal. Praise Jesus, my healer and salvation. Without him, I have nothing. Pulling up my bootstraps now and going to bed.

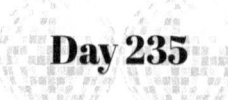

Day 235

"No, in all these things we are more than conquerors
through him who loved us."
Romans 8:37

Hello, *You Don't Need Headlights to Shine*! I'm baaaack! I have missed you. It was very therapeutic to document my daily struggles. The truth is, I haven't been doing that well emotionally or physically, for that

matter. No one prepares you for the AC (after cancer). It's been harder in some ways because I'm done, right? I'm healed. I'm back in the saddle. Wrong! But that's what people assume or

people expect. I am on two chemo pills. I started taking one during radiation, and I thought it was pretty bad until I started taking the second chemo, and that one made the first one look like Tic-tac's. Let's call that one the Dragon because it's constantly dragging me to the bathroom. I've had almost uncontrollable diarrhea and severe nausea. It feels just like I'm back on chemo, except now I'm expected to work and be normal, right? I mean, no one really expects me to be normal; they just don't realize it's not quite over yet. I guess I didn't, either. I still have weekly doctor appointments and I have to have a partial hysterectomy.

I met with the gynecologist today to schedule the hysterectomy. I thought I was used to being poked and prodded, but today was a rude awakening. I had a pelvic exam, which these days I'm used to lots of people seeing my boobs, so the exam wasn't that much more uncomfortable until….. the doc said to take in a deep breath, and as she was telling me what to expect, she does it!! A RECTAL EXAM!!! My God!! I was not ready! And she did not need to tell me to inhale because that's exactly what you automatically do! I gasped for air! I swear I felt her elbow inside me. As horrible as it was, it was over in seconds, and she was gone lickety-split!! She threw some paper towels at me and told me to clean up and get dressed so that she would be back. I sat there paralyzed. Stunned. What just happened? My butt is THROB-BING! Did she leave something in there?!? My God! I think I need to sit on a donut. I come out of my daze, clean all the lubricant off and dress myself. Still, I sat there waiting for her to return, and I was paralyzed with shock. That had to be hands down the most unpleasant thing to date. I gather my thoughts just before she returns and we discuss my robotic BSO surgery (Bilateral Salpingo-Oophorectomy).

I'll have my tubes and ovaries removed. They'll use the same incisions from my gallbladder surgery and my recovery will be minimal. I cannot drive under any circumstances for 4-6 weeks. She says abdominal muscles are used when we drive and she doesn't let her patients drive because you can develop hernias. I don't even have abdominal muscles. As soon as I feel up to it, I can work because standing and walking around as much as possible will help me recover. Just no heavy lifting. I am so relieved that I won't need a ton of time off work again. After the surgery, I will be able to stop the monthly Lupron shots that suppress my estrogen, so I'll only be taking the two oral chemo pills. One month down, 23 to go for the Dragon.

Lots has happened during the last two months while I haven't written. I think I'm trying to figure out my new normal. And until this point everything has been scripted out. Today, I feel hopeful again that things are getting better. During my hiatus, I met with my plastic surgeon for the very last time before he handed me over to a new Dr. My plastic surgeon deserves the best retirement in the world. He may not always remember me, but I will never forget him. The new Dr will see me in December to discuss the future of Sponge Blob. SB has been so much better. He stays put a lot more, so I'm pretty sure I'll just need the fat grafting to add tissue to my breasts. I have no idea where they'll harvest fat from; I can't possibly have any to spare, but all this is to be decided next year: new deductible.

God is always with me. I have never felt alone on this journey. But He is very quiet. I don't have a lot to say to Him lately either, but I rest in His perfect peace. When I cannot utter a prayer, I know the Holy Spirit intercedes for me, so let's just say the Holy Spirit has been working overtime lately. I know I will have highs and lows and that's ok. But I have never felt like Jesus wasn't there. I'm so thankful for His unconditional love for me.

Day 237

*"Many are the affiliations of the righteous, but the Lord
delivers him out of them all."*
Psalm 34:19

Heartburn, nausea, diarrhea…no, this isn't a Pepto Bismol advertisement. It's the ugly side of chemo. I've talked about everything else here, so why not poop? It's my reality. And it's not fun at all. I cannot get this under control. I can't seem to find a happy medium. And yes. For the next 23 months, it will be this way. I may learn to manage it better, but the Dragon messes with your GI tract. I sat down to research all the reasons I was not able to take this crap (literally) anymore so I could present it to my doctor. But what I found are all the reasons why I should take it. And Suck. It. Up. There is such a high chance of cancer returning. This is why Doc is putting me through this. I saw it for myself as I read Every. Single. Report. From day one of diagnosis all the way to the present day, I read all the raw factors that dictated my treatment and why it made sense. My age, the number and size of my masses, the fact that it had spread to my lymph nodes, the growth stage etc. etc., I also enjoyed reading what a pleasant patient I am, which helped to boost my ego a little bit. But anyway, back to business. I will have good days and bad days, and I will learn a new way of life in the next 23 months. It's a short time to suffer, hoping I never do this again. I can't imagine hearing the words "it's back" all because I couldn't handle a little poop. Some days, I can't be far from the bathroom; some days, I figure it out. And to top it off, I have my first UTI. I know it's from that aggressive pelvic exam I had on Friday. My body went into a state of shock! It's awful. I have a newfound sympathy for chronic sufferers. In writing this, I hope to look back on it very soon and be able to say that I have all this managed. I know there's a reason for all of this, and it'll work out.

Day 241

For it is God who works in you to act in order
to fulfill his good purpose.
Philippians 2:13

My hysterectomy is scheduled. The procedure is called a BSO. I will have my fallopian tubes and ovaries removed. They are directly connected to the carotid artery, so there are risks, but of course, they doesn't anticipate any. Removing these will eliminate the monthly shot I have to go to Moffitt for. I'm most excited that I won't miss much work since I'm finally getting back in the swing of things. She said after a couple of weeks, I can work as soon as I feel like it. Being up and about helps remove all the gas from surgery and promotes healing. I cannot lift or drive for 6 weeks. That's it! She will use the same incisions from my gallbladder surgery and remove any scar tissue from that procedure. I'm so glad to have this part planned out and almost checked off the list.

Today I saw my cancer surgeon. I love her so much. We chatted and laughed for a long time before getting to my appointment. She has released me to come every six months. I will never have a mammogram, just palpate exams. Checking for any new lumps or bumps. And, of course, I am to do self-checks as well. Everything looks great and we are both happy with how things turned out aesthetically. She told me that it would take at least a year for me to get back to 'normal', which would all be new. She, a BC survivor herself, said I will never truly be the same, but that doesn't mean it's bad. And since I'm still taking therapy drugs, I have to give myself even longer. It's a relief to hear her say that. I feel so much pressure to be my old self. No one is putting that pressure on me in particular, I just feel it. It's ok to feel sick and tired and it's ok to take naps, which is all I needed to hear. I love my naps.

Day 242

"Humble yourselves, therefore, under God's mighty hand, that he may lift you up in due time. Cast all your anxiety on him because he cares for you. Be alert and of sober mind. Your enemy the devil prowls around like a roaring lion looking for someone to devour. Resist him, standing firm in the faith, because you know that the family of believers throughout the world is undergoing the same kind of sufferings. And the God of all grace, who called you to his eternal glory in Christ, after you have suffered a little while, will himself restore you and make you strong, firm and steadfast. To him be the power for ever and ever. Amen."
1 Peter 5:6-11

I can't believe I ever worry about anything. I'm not a huge worrier, to begin with. But God really does have everything under control. If we can just sit back and let it unfold, that is true faith. I'm trying really hard to just sit back. Worry does nothing for the situation at hand. It doesn't make it better or make it happen faster. All it does is put a wedge between us and God. When He says, 'Cast all your cares,' He really means it. Every single stupid care in the world can fit on His shoulders. So, why is it so hard to hand them over? No faith. I look back at all the strife I have had as a mom and think how silly. Of course, now it's easy to have faith when things are looking good. But I am working on having faith when things don't look so good because there's never been a time in my life when He didn't come through.

Day 243

But he said to me, "My grace is sufficient for you, for my power is made perfect in weakness." Therefore I will boast all the more gladly of my weaknesses, so that the power of Christ may rest upon me.
2 Corinthians 12:9

I've been to Moffitt 5 out of the last 10 days. I have so many labs and scans and different doctors who want to check different things. That also includes a trip to urgent care for my

UTI. I really like the PA at my oncology office. She's young and very knowledgeable. I think we'd be friends in the real world, we talk about hair and motherhood and life. She's very

thorough when it comes to monitoring me on the Dragon. There are tons of things it does to your body. Besides the diarrhea, she's concerned with my white count, it's low. It really messes with your immune system. I need to be really careful not to catch anything. I have to stop taking it for my hysterectomy because it can interfere with healing. That will be nice to have a break from the diarrhea while I'm healing.

She's also worried about my headaches and dizziness. I chalked it up to my lack of nutrition with all the nausea, but she wants me to have a brain MRI just to be sure. I'll also have another scan for the spot on my spleen to see how that looks after the last six months. If I get sick in any way, a cold or a fever, I am to stop taking the Dragon and call my nurse immediately. I'm a "sickly" person now in my eyes. I'm not healthy like I've always been. It's a hard pill to swallow, literally. I take 17 pills a day. I had to get an am/pm pill sorter. And in the morning, I'm so nauseated that my body wants to reject my pills. It's so hard to get them down.

My surgical oncologist said I'll be a new "me" when this is all over. I can already see what she means. I feel fragile and unbreakable all at the same time. I'm weak but strong, tired but tireless. I really can't wait to tick off the years one by one until official remission is here.

It's time for school to start and I have never been more removed from a situation in my life. I've always been so prepared for events. Now, I feel like I'm in a bubble, but everything around me carries on without me. Thank God Presley has a job and ordered all of her school clothes. Harper, on the other hand, has nothing. She wears uniforms, if you want to even call them that. I didn't even know when her open house was scheduled. I feel so out of the loop. Her open house is at the same time as my pre-op appointment, and I feel so bad that I can't be there with her. I can't believe the carefree days of summer are almost gone. My prayer is for the school year to go smoothly because I just really have no energy to engage.

Day 245

*"For our light and momentary troubles are achieving for us
an eternal glory that far outweighs them all. So we fix our
eyes not on what is seen, but on what is unseen, since what
is seen is temporary, but what is unseen is eternal."*
2 Corinthians 4:17-18

Ok, I gotta come up with a code word for this diarrhea since it's part of my life now. I think I've decided to call it "the gym." I hate the gym, and I hate diarrhea, so henceforth, I shall refer to the unwanted visitor as the gym. I went to the gym at 3am and again at 5am. By 9 am, I was on my third Imodium. I can take up to eight a day. Lord, please don't ever let me have to do that. Even if I can get the gym under control, I still have a lot of discomfort and nausea. Some days, I do better than others. Some days, one pill will do to keep the gym away. It's so confusing because you never really know what to expect. On a good day, I feel like going to the gym is the least I can do if it prevents cancer from returning. On my worst days, I'm so sick of the gym I want to give up completely. I did the research. I know I have to keep going to the gym. I know each day the results will be different, but I have to keep chugging along. Two months down, 22 to go.

While I don't believe this verse is talking about going to the gym, I do believe that my suffering is for a moment, and God will get the glory through my gym membership. When I look at my situation from eternity's perspective, I will never have to go to the gym again.

Day 246

*"Trust in the Lord with all your heart and lean not on
your own understanding; in all your ways submit to him,
and he will make your paths straight."*
Proverbs 3:5-6

I can't stay out of the gym this morning. It's still early, so I have time to get things under control before my first client. Right now, I feel like calling my nurse and telling her we have to cut my dosage in half. At my last visit, she told me that was an option. I would still take it for two years; I wouldn't have to take it longer. I'm going to message her right now before I change my mind. I sent her a message. I'm on my third Imodium, tums and Zofran for nausea and I have to work in two hours. I am MISERABLE! I don't know how people with intestinal issues survive. If I reschedule clients, I have nowhere to put them on my schedule, so I've got to figure this out. Most of the time, once I get involved with a client, it helps to distract me from how I'm feeling.

I just had a meltdown. I made the decision not to take my chemo this morning. I just don't see how I'd ever get out of the gym to work. It's a very bad day. I am just not doing well. It's really the first time in the two months that I've been mentally and physically defeated. I just can't today.

It's a full moon. Go figure. So, my doctor is on vacay, but her PA won't lower my dose until I am maxed out on eight Imodium pills a day. The thing is, even if I avoid the gym, I still have massive cramps.

My plastics nurse came in this morning for her hair appointment, and we discussed that I have taken every precaution for my cancer not to return. She thinks that if I am unable to take the Dragon, it's not the end of the world. At some point, I need to have a quality of life. I've been an MIA parent lately because of this. And I think she's right. I have done every single preventative measure so far. For now, I will take one dose a day, just nightly, and see if I can manage that way. If not, I will not go back on it after my hysterectomy.

Day 247

"The Lord is my shepherd, I lack nothing."
Psalm 23:1

Yesterday, I was pretty low. I had to cancel some clients after all. Today is the second day that I will not take my morning chemo. I've got to see if I can find a way to function better before I give up completely. But my nurse friend is right. I have done everything preventative possible. And a few years ago, the Dragon wasn't even an option. So, I can't look at it as not doing everything possible to prevent re-occurrence because I have. Now that I've had that realization, I'm at peace with stopping the meds completely if this dosage drop doesn't help. I'm tired of being disconnected from my family and the world. I usually am up to date on all the world events and I can't say the last time I even heard what's going on in the world.

Day 248

"Blessed is the one who does not walk in step with the wicked or stand in the way that sinners take or sit in the company of mockers."
Psalm 1:1

Day two of 1/2 chemo dose and I can tell a difference. Still not 100% but I can see a silver lining. I have no idea what I wrote yesterday. I was pretty bad. I know it was a lot of complaining because I was pretty low. Today was such an improvement, but I am without energy and can barely make it by the afternoon. My visits to the gym are more managed and the doc is just going to have to accept my terms. I did get some medical education at Grey Sloan Memorial Hospital via Greys Anatomy. Not much in the oncology department, but enough to know when it's been enough. I'm needing some energy to get a few craft projects done that I'm looking forward to. I finally put out the bird bath that I made with thrifted items (I'm an old lady). And I'm going to start making candles! Already bought my starter kit.

But after I finish a day of work, I am worthless. With all the holidays around the corner, I have to have the energy to decorate my house. It's one of my favorite things.

Day 249

"But whose delight is in the law of the Lord and who meditates on His law day and night, that person is like a tree planted by streams of water."
Psalm 1:2-3

I'm starting to feel human again. I can't believe how bad I let myself get before intervening on my own behalf. Day three on a half dose of the Dragon. I don't see how I could ever go back. This may actually be sustainable for the duration. It's still not ideal, and my body will not adjust, but I could deal with how things seem to be. After the last three days, I looked back, and I'm just so mad that I let myself be so sick without thinking I am in control of my medical decisions. Until this point, I've done every single thing each doctor has recommended. I did good. I'm not a martyr. I won't get a medal or some prize money at the end. When I was pregnant, people would ask if I planned on getting an epidural. Of course!! Why wouldn't I? There's no trophy or recognition for doing it naturally! Same with this, I don't need to put myself through torture just to say I did it.

We had dinner with all of our neighbors tonight. It was the first time I'd tried to eat an actual meal in a while. I've been getting by on the brat diet pretty much. I took Imodium beforehand and I was good at dinner. We had a lot of laughs. I was able to eat a little bit of salad, a baked potato, and two bites of steak. Food sits so heavy in my stomach. It's a very unpleasant feeling. Like I overate except I didn't. I was ok until we got home, and I had to take the Dragon, and then I was off to the gym again. During the day, I eat a granola bar or a peanut butter cracker. It's not good for me to continue like that, but I just can't stomach anything. Especially if I'm working, Imodium doesn't stop the cramps. Anyway, all this complaining makes me depressed. I'm going to bed and hoping tomorrow I can get some stuff done around the house that I won't be able to get done after my surgery.

Day 250

*"Praise be to the God and Father of our Lord Jesus Christ,
the father of compassion and the God of all comfort who
comforts us in all our troubles so that we can comfort those
in any trouble with the comfort we ourselves receive from
God."*
2 Corinthians 1:3-4

I have gone to the gym in my sleep. It's 2:30 am and I wake up sick. I can't believe this happened while I was sleeping. I shower and clean everything, all while Chad snores away. Thank God I sleep on a lumbar pillow and that is the only thing that is dirty. I take two more Imodium. I took one at dinner last night and one before I went to bed. I knew it was too good to be true. Eating somewhat of an actual meal makes things so much worse. I'm back in bed now. In the morning, I'll bleach all of our bedding just to be sure. It should be fun telling Chad about my fiasco while he was sound asleep through it all. He's been working long hours, so I'm glad he slept through my debacle. I'm going to try to get some sleep of my own now.

Back at the gym this morning by 8am. I have lots to do today besides bleaching everything in the bedroom. As much as I hate my situation, it has not broken me yet. I think I may be numb. I haven't lost hope or feel that I'm at the end of my rope yet. Can you imagine? I have pooped the bed in my sleep, and I'm not freaking out! What's wrong with me? I'm scared to see what my breaking point is! I feel like I should be at my wit's end. In some ways, I am, but I almost feel like this isn't where I'll be for long. I feel like there's something for me just around the corner that will change all of this madness. My prayers these days are equivalent to that look you give your best friend when something crazy just happened, "Like, really!?! Did that just happen?" I don't even pray words; it just looks like I give the Holy Spirit to deliver to Jesus. He'll know what they mean. Maybe I am at the end of my rope, I am crying writing this because I'm tired of it. I'm so weak physically and my brain has all these ideas and activities planned, but I just can't seem to muster the motivation I need. I can't wait to come off the Dragon for my upcoming surgery. I'll probably go through some kind of nesting period where I'll feel the need to get my life together again.

Day 252

"Rejoice in the Lord always. I will say it again: rejoice!
Let your gentleness be evident to all. The Lord is near. Do
not be anxious about anything, but in every situation,
by prayer and petition, with thanksgiving, present your
requests to God."
Phillipians 4:4-6

It's just too hot outside. It zaps any energy I may have. My trips to the gym have been less frequent between yesterday and today. Maybe the lower dosage is making a difference. My oncologist is back from vacation and she messaged me that she agreed with the PA that I should not lower my dose of the Dragon until I'm taking eight Imodium a day. Or she can call me in a prescription for diarrhea medication. No thanks. This is better. I can't imagine what all this has done to my GI tract. I'm not sure when I'll tell her I lowered the dose, probably the next time I see her. I still have very low energy unless I can fit in a nap. I had the busiest week so far last week and I was worn out. I do feel like I'm able to be more present mentally to what's going on around me. I am 5 pounds away from my pre-chemo pre-steroid weight. Although that's not the most fun way to lose weight I am glad to have that accomplished.

Day 254

The Lord your God is with you, the Mighty Warrior who
saves. He will take great delight in you;
Zephaniah 3:17

Everything hurts. I'll blame chemo for most of it. My pectoral muscles hurt. I've finally used them for the first time since they were scraped and scooped out. I lifted a piece of furniture and they're so sore now. Then, my ears hurt and I'm not sure I'm 100% over the UTI. My emotions are out of control. I'm raging one minute and crying the next. I know my family thinks I'm lazy and all I do is lay on the couch, but frankly, I don't ever feel good. I'm so worn down and I'm tired of feeling this way. After about four hours of working, I need a break. I'm not always able to do that so I press on. I'm frequenting the gym a lot less and also taking way less Imodium. I feel like I'm coming out of a fog and I think that's why I'm so emotional. I can see what I've been missing.

I'm very much looking forward to a good school year with maybe some fun sprinkled in here and there. I'm just not me. I don't feel good at any time. I don't go around complaining; I save that for here. But I am never normal; I just go with it. And since I don't talk about it nonstop, my family assumes I'm fine, which, for the most part, I carry on with my regular activities. I want to be in bed almost 24/7. But I'm a doer. When it comes to house duties, I can't rest until things are done. I've always been able to keep up with laundry and cleaning through this whole thing. I've had people offer to clean my house and do the chores but the truth is I'd have to be completely bedridden before I'd take up the offer. So, I guess what I'm trying to say is that I never feel good, but life goes on, and I know it's temporary, but it would sure be nice if I could be normal soon. I'm sure a lot of this is the sudden shock of menopause my body is going through. I've heard women say how awful it is and how they don't feel themselves.

Day 260

"We all like sheep have gone astray, each of us has turned to our own way; and the Lord has laid on him the iniquity of us all."
Isaiah 53:6

I recently realized that Sponge Blob has been a nonissue. My skin has tightened just like my beloved plastic surgeon said it would. SB can still flip 360* but not without help, so he stays in place. I've been so focused on feeling cruddy that I hadn't noticed this one improvement! Now all I will need next year is fat grafting to help add tissue and shape to Tweedle D and Tweedle Double D.

I am still only taking one dose daily of my bad chemo and the doctor still doesn't know. This Thursday, I will stop it completely before my surgery next week. I will decide what to do after recovery. I'm also realizing that part of the cruddy feeling I have must be menopause. Being thrown into it without any ease has made me crazy. I've heard horror stories over the years from women describing the symptoms. Now I know firsthand. It makes your mind crazy, your body weird and exhausted and I'm very irritable.

I've been awake since 3am and I'm uncomfortable in my own skin. It feels terrible. And I'm honest when people ask how I'm doing. I'm an official old lady who declares all of her aches and pains to whoever will listen. But I have to be honest because I don't want people to assume I'm able to function as my old self. I don't want the expectation on me. I do all of my normal activities and functions, just at a lower capacity. On the rare occasion that I go my normal rate, I pay for it later.

When I was two years old, I started getting migraines (hereditary) and by four, I was officially diagnosed. Over the years, they ebbed and flowed depending on puberty and my cycle. I would go years and not have one. Now, they are back routinely. I feel it's the menopause crap. It's just really fun and exciting to see what is around the corner every day. Will it be my hip today? Or maybe a burning UTI. How about uncontrollable visits to the gym? Will I go to the gym in my sleep again? It's ok, though. Truly, this is all for documentation purposes so that when I am a real old lady, I can look back and count the years of survival.

Tonight, I ran into some friends I've known for years. They're a little older than me and past menopause. They were at their little ladies' supper club, and out of the eight or so women, three were long-time breast cancer survivors. It was so reassuring to look into their faces and see that they were completely normal, fun-loving women after their battle. One said to me it changes your life, but not always for the worst. And I had to agree. I wouldn't change my journey, but I sure am anxious to get to the point where I can look back on it years and years later. I'm so thankful that I've learned that I can truly give my worries and fears to Jesus, and I have gotten so much better about not picking them up again. It's so weird to be tied to sickness but also have a freeing feeling of no worry in the world. Of course, I stress about my small business and my kids, but at the end of every day, I am ok. Really and truly.

Day 265

"Praise be to the Lord, to God our Savior,
who daily bears our burdens."
Psalm 68:19

Everything takes more energy than I have or more mental focus than I can give. I'm worried that this time period of me being disengaged will have severe repercussions. The last nine months have been full of disruption for all of us and I'm not sure how many more months will pass before I am able to resume a new normal. It's pretty clear that I will never be my old self and I'm at peace with that. But I wish my family could see inside my brain and the absolutely insane mess that it is. I wish I could wear a sign that says stay back 200 feet. Or now is a good time to approach. Or please stop asking me questions and my head's going to explode. I have no control over my emotions or the overwhelming feeling I get sometimes, and I never have warning of when I'm going to lose it. I'm a mess, just barely holding it together at times, for no reason at all but for all the reasons. Diagnosis, surgery and treatment seemed so much easier than whatever this is. It's like I'm losing my mind, but there's not an actual reason for it. Except there is, I guess.

At the beginning of it all, I was in control of my emotions, and I was on top of things for the most part. Now it's spiraling out of control and I can't see where I lost it. I know it's menopause. And I'm hoping surgery will bring stability to my mind and body. I feel like an absolute lunatic lives inside me and I'm continually trying to suppress her. What can I name her? She needs a name so I can talk about her when she's acting a fool. I hate it when she shows up. I want to tell her to get a grip and stop crying or raging or whatever she's doing at the moment. I want her to stop having pity parties. No one cares. Everyone has their own crap to deal with.

My mother named me Kathleen. Kathleen seems too refined or

proper. (not me at all). Thank God once I was born, my aunt came to the hospital to meet me and instantly nicknamed me Katie. My whole family calls me Katie or Kate. So maybe I shall call the crazy old lady in my head Kathleen. It's been hours since Kathleen had her reign. After a nap, I feel much better. But that doesn't mean that she won't show up at the first challenge I face. I know a solution to this whole mess. A personal assistant. But unfortunately, I married for love and not money, so I will not be getting an assistant.

Day 266

"And so we know and rely on the love God has for us. God is love. Whoever lives in love lives in God, and God in them."
1 John 4:16

Kathleen never made an appearance today. She's been hanging around for days, weeks even. I thought she might show herself at my MRI today. I had to talk her down. I had forgotten how scary they can be, but I kept my eyes closed and pushed away thoughts of being buried alive. The scans today are revisiting the spot on my spleen and seeing if there's another reason other than heredity or menopause for the migraines.

Day 267

"I eagerly expect and hope that I will no way be ashamed,
but will have sufficient courage so that now as always
Christ will be exalted in my body, whether by life or
whether by death."
Philippians 1:20

The surprises just keep coming! My oncologist PA called me just now with the results from my scans yesterday. She started out with "Well the good news is the spot on your spleen went from 1.1-.09 and we still think it's benign."

That's great! So, that means there's bad news? God, what now? I have a cholesterol granuloma on the right side of my brain. It's a type of cyst. She says they're usually benign. It wasn't there before. So, she's sending me to a neurosurgeon because sometimes they want to take them out. This may be causing my migraines to flare up and the dizziness I've had. She said it also is on the nerve of my inner ear. It makes sense that I've had ear and jaw pain since chemo.

Soooooooooooooooooooooooooo Good times. I feel like I should be on disability with the amount of doctor's appointments I have. So now that makes a team of six doctors, including my GP and their PAs, on top of that. It's almost comical to have 12 medical pros who think they all need to see me for themselves. Anyway, I'm pretty numb to this news right now. I think in the grand scheme it's probably nothing. But if the headaches and dizziness don't go away, then what? I can't go there right now.

Day 268

"For it is by grace you have been saved, through faith - and this is not from yourselves, it is the gift of God."
Ephesians 2:8

SpongeBlob has flipped, and I can't get him to go back. The flat side of my dome shaped implant is facing outward. My skin has tightened a lot more and now it's harder to manipulate SB. It must've happened in my sleep. The cavity underneath is still so tender that I can't flip him back like he should be. I'm so aggravated because I don't see my new plastic surgeon until December and I really don't want to spend the next several months with SB. Tomorrow is surgery day. I'm excited for several reasons. Firstly, I'll be at the newest state-of-the-art hospital. Secondly, I'm looking forward to some downtime and extra rest. Thirdly, I'm hoping surgery will put some kind of end to the menopause madness. I am not nervous at all. People keep asking me if I'm stressed about it and I'm honestly not. I feel like the mastectomy went so well, and that's considered a major surgery; this seems so insignificant compared. All I need now is to shower with my lovely Hibiclens cleanse surgery soap and hit the sack, ready for tomorrow.

Day 269

"Blessed is the one who perseveres under trial because,
having stood the test, that person will receive the crown of
life that the Lord has promised to those who love him."
James 1:12

Surgery day. I'm up and ready to get this going. I took a deep breath this morning and flipped Sponge Blob. I'm so glad the poor nurse who undresses me for surgery doesn't have to see him. I kept imagining her face once she removed my gown and there was this huge, square, nippleless blob lying there. Now, it won't be so much of a shock for her. And I never eat breakfast, but of course, I'm starving because I'm not allowed to eat. Arrival time was 9:45am and they didn't take me back until 2. So, it was a very long day for both Chad and me. But the surgery went as expected and I woke up with minimal pain. I haven't taken any pain meds since I've been home. I just have soreness. My kidney levels were not that great so they don't want me taking ibuprofen. Tylenol is what I'll have. I won't need the narcotic they prescribed. All I wanted to do was sleep off the anesthesia.

Day 271

"I know that my redeemer lives, and that in the end He will stand on earth."
Job 19:25

I swore I didn't have any ab muscles, but apparently, I do because they hurt! I am so sore! I have to hand it to any cesarean section survivors because I don't even want to move. This isn't like gallbladder surgery at all or even the mastectomy. Stomach muscles are involved in everything you do! I can see why she doesn't want me to drive for so long. I think I would be scared to. It's not an encompassing pain, just super uncomfortable, and it makes me want to sit still, which is exactly what they said not to do. But I'm scared to disrupt anything if I move too much. Prescription Tylenol isn't really helping much, so I took a tramadol. I didn't notice a difference with that, except it made me dizzy, so I went to bed at about 8:30pm. It's really not so bad. I've been through worse. But I don't like being dependent on someone else to take me places. Of course, I want to shop, and walking would be good for me, so we'll see if I can do that today.

Day 275

Even though I walk through the darkest valley,
I will fear no evil, for you are with me;
your rod and your staff, they comfort me.
Psalm 23:4

We dodged another hurricane; thank you, Lord. It's been too much for me and now Kathleen is here. Her depressive ways have taken over. I want to be a recluse. No talking, no questions, no interaction. It's a terrible way to be. I have no idea what makes her show up or what makes her leave.

I can't explain the emptiness I feel. I have that feeling of uncomfortableness in my own skin. I want to be able to close my eyes and be past all this when I open them again. There's absolutely no reason for me to feel so awful except that my body has to do its thing. I remember, as a kid, my mom talking about wanting to get a hotel and room service for herself. Now I get it. Except I'm not running away from anything. I want to run away from me, from Kathleen. There's no escaping this; I just have to let my body get through it. To my knowledge, there's not much I can do to speed things along.

After my shower, I felt a little better. I can't stand to read the truths I've written. It's such a dark and lonely place to be at times. And even though I have a hope and a peace that only Christ can give, I still go through these periods of emptiness. I know with all certainty that He's in control; even in my darkest moments, I don't forget that. That's what makes it so weird. That's why I want to crawl out of my body at times. I know my foundation isn't rattled, so why is my mind so crazy? I'm going to have to contact my doctor just to see if there's something she thinks I can do. She's also going to want to know if I'm taking my chemo again and the answer is no. I should start it tomorrow, but I can't bear the thought of it. I'm feeling so much better physically and my incision sites are not nearly as sore. The bruising is clearing up as well. I'm almost normal again. Maybe the subconscious thought that I need to resume treatment is making me unsettled, too. All I know is that Kathleen is not welcome to stick around, and as soon as I can figure out how I'm getting her out of my life.

Day 280

"The Lord has heard my cry for mercy; the Lord accepts my prayer"
Psalm 6:9

I've learned that you can't put limits on God. The days that I don't feel Him has nothing to do with Him being near me or not. He is within me. My ability to feel his presence does not limit what he can do. God is not a "feeling" to me. He is a fact; he is the truth. The Holy Spirit dwells within me. He NEVER leaves. The Bible says He is with me until the end of the ages. I can't let my emotions limit my perception of what I feel God is doing in my life. It's like a friendship with someone you don't see often, but they'll always be your friend. And when you're together, it's amazing, and it's like you were never apart. It's like that with God for me. I don't always feel his presence, but when I do, it's like we've never been apart. So weird and hard to explain. That's the part of my journey where I have to learn to trust Him more. Even when He's quiet, I know he's close. Even when Kathleen is around, He's right there too. She hasn't been around for days and I'm so grateful. I feel almost human again between healing from surgery and being free from the Dragon. I've been eating salad again!! And I don't want to give that up! I haven't decided what I'll do about taking chemo again because I haven't let myself think about it. It's like I'm waiting for my doctor to call and ask me if I'm doing what I'm supposed to be doing. I haven't even checked to see when my appointment with her is. I'm just relishing this time I have until I figure out what's next. I am still taking the original chemo that I will take for 10 years. I did not get a break from that one, even for surgery. It's once a day and that one causes joint pain. With arthritis in every joint, it exacerbates the joint pain. I'm pretty accustomed to the feeling. Sometimes, I'm stiff if I've been standing/sitting for too long. As much as it hurts and I feel like an old lady, I can go on with it. But the Dragon, ugh. It's only two years but the gastrointestinal issues are next level.

I have friends with IBS and even Crohn's disease. They don't have a two-year limit on the effects. I don't know how people survive it.

While the storm raged on, Jesus was sound asleep on the boat, while the disciples worried and fretted about it. Jesus was confident His Father was in control. While some kind of chaos is sure to find me every single day, I can relax in the steadfastness of my Father.

Day 287

Yet you, Lord, are our father. We are the clay, you are the potter; we are all the work of your hand.
Isaiah 64:8

In seventh grade, my science teacher made us memorize all 206 bones in the body. I can't remember the majority of them anymore, but I can tell you all 206 of mine hurt. I hurt from head to toe. I don't even remember what it's like to not hurt. I ache constantly, and I have weird, random things come up: skin irritation, a random lump or bump, hot flashes, and, of course, the surprising cameos from Kathleen. I'm so over it. When I'm "normal," I'm not really normal. I'm just accustomed to feeling terrible, so I roll with it. There are occasions when I feel less terrible, but it's still terrible. My mind still wants to go and do things like my old normal self and for the majority of the time, I can. I push myself a lot because I know I would feel the same if I stayed home to rest, so I might as well do things I enjoy. But I am tired. So sick and tired of all of it.

This past weekend was very busy. I loved every minute of it, but my body was not happy. I hate complaining about it as much as I hate dealing with it. I've become one of those old ladies who talk about her ailments all the time. But I can relate. It's unbelievable how awful you can feel and still just keep chugging along. This morning at Walgreens, a man was headed toward the exit, hunched over his walker and with his wife at his side. As I walked inside, I heard the painful cries of the man. Deep groans and loud outbursts. He could barely move. I assumed he had been to the pharmacy at the back of the store and could not make it back to the car. It was a pitiful sight. The cashier called for a manager to help. The closer the man got to the door, the louder his cries became. And even once they got him to the car, he was screaming out in horrible pain. I feel like they should've called an ambulance. Was he being a dramatic man? Or was he really that bad off? I don't know, but I said a prayer for him anyway. At this rate, that could be me when I'm his age; I feel so old already. As I write this, it's 2am, and I cannot sleep, so I check my email.

"Welcome to Medicare" are the first words I see. Even the universe knows I'm old.

Day 288

"Yes, and I will continue to rejoice, for I know
that through your prayers and God's provision of the
Spirit of Jesus Christ what has happened to me will
turn out for my deliverance."
Philippians 1:18-19

This morning I had a post-op Zoom call with my OB, who performed my surgery. She asked if I had been driving. I lied straight to her face. Of course, I have driven some. I'm a mom. Things come up. She's worried driving can cause a hernia, but I don't have a hernia. I have accidentally lifted things before remembering I shouldn't. But other than that, I'm doing fine, and she wants to see me in person in 3 weeks. I still have not resumed taking the Dragon and I will see my oncologist next week. I'm going to have to start taking it probably tonight so that when I do see her I can speak genuinely about all the side effects I experience. It's also concerning that the pharmacy calls and sends emails about all the risks involved with taking it. They're constantly asking strange questions like have I had suicidal thoughts, how is my kidney function, do I feel depressed or reclusive? YES!! Not suicidal but depressive, yes. But is it the medicine or the situation? Because until recently, I haven't been in the valley very much. I think this is by far the toughest part of the whole journey. From what other survivors tell me, it's normal to have these feelings. I still have so much support, though. I'm learning from others how to be more compassionate and not just pray for people when I think of them but also let them know it. That has gotten me through so many days, a random message saying someone is thinking about me. And Jesus is right here with me all the time. It's like we are playing the silent game, though, and He's waiting for me to be the one to speak up. But if I speak, I will cry. And I hate to cry. So, we both sit in silence. It's a rotten place to be, but I don't feel helpless or stuck. It's a process I must go through to get to the other side of the mountain.

I reread some of my early journal entries and cried like a baby at God's goodness. So many things I had forgotten. He gave me so many words of encouragement and I am grateful for writing them down because now as we play the silent game, I can go back and see all that He has done for me and I know my story is not over.

Day 289

*"Your sun will never set again, and your moon will wane
no more; the Lord will be your everlasting light, and your
days of sorrow will end."*
Isaiah 60:20

I feel like absolute trash today. There are a few new things that could be contributing factors. This will be a continuation of my pity party that started a few days ago. My labs came back from my GP and all of my numbers are completely off. Everything was either too high or too low, including my blood counts. So that alone can cause my crappy feeling. And the right side of my skull is throbbing. Is it from that cyst? Who even knows at this point? And I still have this strange lump on my left arm. I can't remember if I documented my arm pain after surgery or not. But a few days after the hysterectomy, my left arm was so tender to the touch that every time I looked at it, I was surprised there were no bruises. It was slightly swollen and I figured it may have had something to do with my IV. Now, almost three weeks later, it's still so tender I can't stand my watch to touch it. My GP doesn't know anything about my new ailments so it should be interesting to hear what she thinks about it all. And I think I should name the cyst. I usually refer to it as my brain tumor, but it's not actually a tumor.

Day 292

*"Be completely humble and gentle; be patient, bearing with
one another in love. Make every effort to keep the unity of
the Spirit through the bond of peace. Then we will no longer
be infants, tossed back and forth by the waves, and blown
here and there by every wind of teaching and by the cunning
and craftiness of people in their deceitful scheming. Instead,
speaking the truth in love, we will grow to become in every
respect the mature body of him who is the head, that is,
Christ. Be kind and compassionate to one another, forgiving
each other, just as in Christ God forgave you."*
Ephesians 4:2-3, 14-15, 32

Today marks one month without the Dragon. I decided to start
taking it tonight. I figured I need to give it one more shot especially
before I see my oncologist Friday.

Day 294-295

"Being confident of this, that he who began a good work in you will carry it on to completion until the day of Christ Jesus."
Philippians 1:6

Barely 24 hours back on chemo, and I feel worse than crap. I almost forgot how bad it actually was. I had a doctor's appointment this morning with my GP and I came home and laid on the couch the rest of the day. Doc did my labs again, and they are still not good. Lots of things could be making me feel terrible on top of chemo. She ordered some meds for me, and I will see what my oncologist says about all this on Friday. I can't write much when I feel like this. I haven't even started going to the gym yet, but I know it's coming. My stomach is cramping. I assume by tomorrow or Wednesday at the latest, I'll be back to that routine.

I started the "gym" today, and I feel awful. I don't want to write when I only have complaints, but I know I need to document things as they are. This morning, I took a two-hour nap. Chad and I collectively decided that I didn't need to take the Dragon. It's just not worth feeling this bad for two years. All I want to do is sleep because that's the only way to escape the side effects. I know Doc will want to try another dosage before I stop altogether, but I'm not sure I want to do that either. I'll see what mood I'm in on Friday when I see her. I didn't take it tonight and probably won't take it in the morning. Trying to work with that in my system just isn't feasible. Even though I don't feel the greatest right now, I know I will get better. I have a closer relationship with Jesus and all the rest will fall into place.

Day 296

"So we fix our eyes not on what is seen, but on what is unseen, since what is seen is temporary, but what is unseen is eternal."
2 Corinthians 4:18

It's so hard waking up one day and life as you knew it is gone. I hardly recognize myself anymore. My once long, straight, red hair is now growing back quite gray, and I'm pretty sure it's going to be curly. I'm tired of being tired. I'm tired of taking medicine. I'm tired of seeing countless doctors at this point. I'm just ready to move on. I feel so stuck. I can't even begin to consider how other people far worse than me are doing this. And some people live years with this crap. I am so over it. And I'm sure whoever reads this feels the same. Sick of my pity parties and whining. That's fine, too. I can't stand myself most of the time. I'm ready for Jesus to come get me. Or send me to a deserted island where I'll have a reason to feel as lonely as I do most of the time. And all I keep thinking about is how my girls will remember me. They don't remember when I was there for them for the past 16 and 13 years. They'll remember mom was always sick and bitchy and went to bed at 8pm.

Tomorrow marks one month since my surgery, and if this is all from removing those God-forsaken ovaries, then I regret my decision. I need to go to a support group to get validation of these feelings. I'm hoping a good night's sleep will solve all of this, but I have a feeling it'll be back. I'm not sure if it's just a phase or hormones or clinical depression. I fill my schedule with friends and activities to look forward to. And when I don't have something planned, I don't feel depressed. But stupid things like laundry piled to the ceiling or dishes in the sink can send me over the edge. Is it too much to think that I shouldn't have to deal with mundane things? My love language is acts of service. No one in this house has a clue. I've asked Chad to talk with the girls about stepping up around the house or with their attitudes and he says he has. Several times. But nothing. I want to go away somewhere for a significant amount of time and see if they even notice. I've considered letting everything go to see how long it would take them all to notice. But it would drive me more insane. I'm sure my mom had issues while she was raising us and I was just as oblivious. I should just go to bed.

Day 297

*"I wait for the Lord , my whole being waits, and in
his word I put my hope. I wait for the Lord more than
watchmen wait for the morning, more than watchmen
wait for the morning."*
Psalms 130:5-6

What a difference sleep makes. I still stand behind my feelings from yesterday, but God has given me peace about it. He's working on me while I'm in this waiting period, or "stuck," which is how it feels. I'm not sure what he needs me to learn, so I'm praying that I'll figure it out. Do I still have areas in my life where I'm not trusting him completely? Or is he teaching me to be patient? I hope not. That's the worst. I know I can't waste this "stuck" period on a pity party. I have to use it to grow and mature my faith. He knows my heart, and my foundation is firm, but there must be something specific I'm not letting him take control of. I have tons to work on, so trying to figure out something specific will be hard to do. I have trust beyond anything. I know he can see that. His goodness prevails over every obstacle. I could never turn away from him, no matter what the diagnosis. So I will stop feeling stuck and use my time wisely to grow and learn whatever it is (so many things) he needs me to learn.

Day 298

"Because of the Lord's great love we are not consumed, for his compassions never fail. They are new every morning; great is your faithfulness. I say to myself, "The Lord is my portion; therefore I will wait for him." The Lord is good to those whose hope is in him, to the one who seeks him; it is good to wait quietly for the salvation of the Lord . For no one is cast off by the Lord forever. Though he brings grief, he will show compassion, so great is his unfailing love. Though he brings grief, he will show compassion, so great is his unfailing love."
Lamentations 3:22-26, 31-33

It's always a good day when I get to see my friend Paige. Paige is my pH balancer. She evens me out. Her faith has stood as a testament to so many, and I always look forward to our visits. We can get pretty real and raw about our struggles and so many tears we have shed together. She's a prayer warrior and an incredible cheerleader (not the actual kind; I wouldn't want to crack a hip). She may never know how much I've grown to depend on her quiet spirit and her calm advice. We laugh and also get very serious at times and I love that she is so real and she is so very special to me.

It's been quite a while since I have felt this good. I actually had energy to get through my day, and I wasn't physically hurting too much. I know the power of prayer is strong, and I have so many prayers going up for me 298 days later. Today is proof that He hears us when we call on Him in our suffering. I'm so grateful for my praying friends who petition on my behalf when I'm not able.

The neurosurgeon called to say he revisited my scans and doesn't think we need to do anything right now about the cyst on my brain. Thank God! That's one less doctor I need to report to for now. This is how God works. After all the complaining I did yesterday, once I finished work, I came home to a clean house, clean laundry, and clean patio and Theo and Olive had been fed. Harper had no way of knowing how much that would mean to me, but God did. I made sure she knew how much I appreciated her doing all of that without anyone asking. Just 24 hours ago, I was sulking in my own misery, and today has been the complete opposite.

Day 299

"Even to your old age and gray hairs I am he, I am he who
will sustain you. I have made you and I will carry you; I
will sustain you and I will rescue you."
Isaiah 46:4

I love my oncologist, but boy, is she persistent. I thought I was clear in my wording that I wasn't going to take the Dragon anymore, and maybe I was clear; she just wasn't hearing it. She wants to lower my dosage from 300mg to 200mg. When I decreased it on my own to 150mg, I did much better, but it was still not pleasant. I'd still take it twice a day, which I think is part of the problem. I'm not sure what I'll do. I have options. I can choose not to take it and lie about it and look like a rock star because I'd have zero side effects. I can try what she suggested or I can take 100mg a day and pretend I'm taking the 200mg. Not sure what to do. My plan was for her to accept my resignation and she didn't. Now I'm back to having that stupid pill hanging over my head. My labs were still not the best. But of course, she attributed it to the Dragon (which I haven't been taking regularly, so something else has me out of whack). She also reminded me that my body has been through a lot, and it'll take time to get things settled.

Day 300

*"The Lord will guide you always; he will satisfy your needs
in a sun-scorched land and will strengthen your frame. You
will be like a well-watered garden,
like a spring whose waters never fail."*
Isaiah 58:11

It's almost time for Portraits of Hope, where my picture will be displayed among other survivors at Moffitt for breast cancer awareness month. I got the invitation for the reception and I can't believe I get to be considered a survivor. I'm very excited to meet the others and hear their stories. Within 300 days, God took me from defeat to victory. It's so incredible to look back and remember the day of diagnosis, all the unknowns, to where I am now. I'm not sure why God has given me the grace of moving my journey along while others take so much longer. Maybe because he knows he created me without patience and didn't want to deal with my nagging for very long. But I am so grateful it's only been 300 days. The good days far outweigh the bad. If I could walk away with one thing from my whole experience it's this. God will truly never leave you, not for one nanosecond. I believe He is in me and all around me; it's impossible for Him to leave once you invite him to stay. I wish people knew what I know through experience, but I think it takes an event to wake us up sometimes to realize He is everything we will ever need.

Day 303

"Now he who supplies seed to the sower and bread for food
will also supply and increase your store of seed and will
enlarge the harvest of your righteousness."
2 Corinthians 9:10

There are 3 types of people in life.

1. Encouragers. Which I am happy to say I have the most of these in my life. People that let you know every time you cross their mind and say a prayer for you. I'm trying to be more like them. There are plenty of people I think about and pray for daily so I'm trying to be better about letting them know it.

2. People that I am supposed to encourage and minister to. Which can be anyone and Everyone. It's amazing to think about how God orchestrates every step I take. People in my path daily might be there for me to share Him. I used to think I had to do more than just plant a seed. But sometimes, all we have to do is cultivate the soil. Our job may not be to actually plant the seed but to get someone to be ready to accept the seed. People can be closed off from the idea of God completely and need a softening of their heart to receive the knowledge.

3. Stumbling blocks. The enemy likes us to keep them around, so we can't fulfill our mission. I've kept a few stumbling blocks around in the past because I told myself I was a witness or that I was the only Jesus they would see. When in reality they were just bringing me down. I may have tilled the ground, but no seed would be planted from our relationship. It's ok to cut those relationships out. Someone else is meant to do the planting. I put pressure on myself to be a farmer at times, from tilling the soil to planting, watering and harvesting. But the truth is God doesn't need me to do any of it. Sometimes, we're just called to be the tiller, or the planter or the waterer and sometimes we get to see the harvest and sometimes we don't. It's not our business to know the whole story; it's just our job to be faithful.

Day 308

*"And let us consider how to stir up one another
to love and good works"*
Hebrews 10:24

Tonight, Moffitt held a reception for Portraits of Hope. So many different faces were featured: young, old, male, female, and all races. Each life was turned upside down by breast cancer. One patient read a poem that she wrote. It brought the room to tears. She was only 26 when she was diagnosed. I can't imagine. I was 26 when we started a family. Reading all the inspiring words from other survivors made me feel understood.

Day 310

*"He who finds a wife finds what is good
and receives favor from the Lord."*
Proverbs 18:22

October 4th, 2003, twenty years ago today, I married my crush. And while things aren't perfect, I can honestly say he was made for me. And since he's still grounded from reading my journal I

can say these things without fear of feeding his ego. No one else could put up with me, and no one else could put up with him. He's a wonderful father and provider. No one can say he's not a hard worker. He's a fierce protector, especially to our girls. We were so young when we got together it's easy to see how some couples don't make the long haul. We're very different

people than when we started. We matured together. Marriage is never easy, but we are both committed for the long haul. Some days, you can't always give 100%, and in today's world, people

make it so easy to give up. But marriage is full of ups and downs because that's how life is. So, I sit here 20 years later and see the life we've built, founded in Christ, and I know we're on solid ground and I am extremely blessed. Life ain't so bad.

Day 314

Jesus said, "Let the little children come to me, and do not hinder them, for the kingdom of heaven belongs to such as these."
Matthew 19:14

It's the eve of Presley's birthday, and I am in total shock at how fast time flies. My baby, my firstborn, is almost an adult. She's far from being ready to cut the apron strings, but already, I feel them getting taut. It's too late to worry if I did everything right; her choices are now all her own. She loves Jesus, which is the most important, all else pales in comparison. She will make mistakes and still need guidance, but all the consequences will be hers. How did it happen so fast? I think back to all the times I was too tired or too frustrated to parent like I should have and it's too late now. I trust in the hedge of protection. I've prayed over her since she was born, and I trust my Heavenly Father, who was there for her when I was not at my best. I'm sad now because I know this year will fly by like all the rest and then she will truly be grown up. She's a burst of sunshine on a cloudy day. Of course, she still can't find the ketchup bottle that's right in front of her face and has no clue what her SS number is, but the world will think she's an adult, and I have to be ready for my baby bird to leave the nest.

Day 316

"Above all, love each other deeply, because love covers over a multitude of sins."
1 Peter 4:8

Today, my cup is full. When life drains me, I have those that fill me up. I haven't had one of these days in a while. I feel like my old self until I look in the mirror and see this granny roller set. My hair is definitely gray and super curly. I still tire easily, but today was a good tired. My squad and I went to see the Portraits of Hope photo display at Moffitt. They got to meet my personal valet attendant, Sharon, who was there every day with a smile and a hug, ready to park Chad's beast of a truck. She told me every day I was beautiful and that she showed up just to see what I'd be wearing. She quickly became someone I looked forward to seeing on my "spa" days at the "resort," and today we took our picture together, and she got to meet my friends. I don't get to see her as frequently, but she always brightens my day.

I didn't think going to see my photo would be a big deal to me. I almost canceled but looking back at today and the journey of the last 316 days, I'm so glad to have this full-circle moment. I feel blessed to have so many people in my corner and I know every single one of them would've gone with me today or any of the last 316 days.

But of course, with my cup so full, there has to be something to tip it over. Chemo. My new dosage has been delivered, 100mg morning and night. I took my first dose minutes ago. Without it I have been so much better physically and emotionally. I'm praying that this dosage will be the Goldilocks. Just right. But for now, I'll go to bed with the fullness of the day

Day 320

*"You will hear of wars and rumors of wars, but see to it
that you are not alarmed. Such things must happen, but
the end is still to come. Nation will rise against nation,
and kingdom against kingdom. There will be famines and
earthquakes in various places.
All these are the beginning of birth pains."*
Matthew 24:6-8

Lately, I've been too tired to write. Chemo makes me so tired, but
I have not gone to the gym once! I know as soon as I write these words
that I shouldn't, but I am hopeful that this dosage will work out.

Day 325

"As the Father has loved me, so have I loved you. Now
remain in my love. If you keep my commands, you
will remain in my love, just as I have kept my Father's
commands and remain in his love. I have told you this
so that my joy may be in you and that your joy may be
complete. My command is this: Love each other as I have
loved you. Greater love has no one than this: to lay down
one's life for one's friends. You are my friends if you do what
I command. I no longer call you servants, because a servant
does not know his master's business. Instead, I have called
you friends, for everything that I learned from my Father
I have made known to you. You did not choose me, but I
chose you and appointed you so that you might go and bear
fruit—fruit that will last—and so that whatever you ask
in my name the Father will give you.
This is my command: Love each other."
John 15:1-17

Life comes at you fast. For the most part we all start on equal ground, healthy babies. And as the years go by, life throws lemons. Each of us makes lemonade at different stages. I remember when my first friend got married, the divorce rate was 50%. I looked at all of my friends and thought, "Not us; none of us will have to deal with that." And now, more than 50% of my friends have dealt with divorce. Divorce, disease, death, and miscarriages have all been lemons in our lives. Everyone is going through something all the time. That's life. But why do some get dealt such sour lemons? It's not fair. My mom always said life's not fair. And it isn't. I can say that 100% of the days I thought I couldn't deal with life's lemons, Jesus got me through.

Jesus, sleep, and a new day can change your perspective on these things. And just when I was going to complain, there's always someone who has it worse. My list of prayer needs continues to grow, not for myself but for those I love. Evil lemons creep in, and I want to obliterate them.

Day 330

*"Is anyone among you in trouble? Let them pray. Is anyone
happy? Let them sing songs of praise. Is anyone among you
sick? Let them call the elders of the church to pray over
them and anoint them with oil in the name of the Lord.
And the prayer offered in faith will make the sick person
well; the Lord will raise them up. If they have sinned, they
will be forgiven. Therefore confess your sins to each other
and pray for each other so that you may be healed. The
prayer of a righteous person is powerful and effective."*
James 5:13-16

I spent the day vomiting yesterday. It's my fault. I got out of my
routine. I thought I could just toss down all of my pills at once. It
wasn't bad at first, just a little nausea, but by the end of it I was sure
I'd puke on my new eye doctor. My normal 20-minute exam was an
hour. By the time I got home, I was in so much pain I was sure I had
the flu. Once my system was clear, I realized it was my mistake. I will
never do that again. I'm back to being irritable and hot-tempered, but
still not nearly as bad as the stronger dosage.

I'm learning that worry, stress and fear are signs that I'm not
trusting God in those areas of my life. It's better said than done, but
over the last year or more, I've come to realize that I really don't have
to carry any of those things. If I'm stressed, it's my fault because I'm
not trusting the Lord to take care of things. When I think about the
things I've wasted time worrying about, it makes me sick because,
100% of the time, things worked out. There's always been a solution.
It may not have always worked out the way I imagined or hoped, but
I'm still here, still chugging along. The burdens I'm carrying now for
those I love are not of worry or fear but of urgency to have relief for
them.

After all, we are never promised days without pain or sorrow.

Daniel wasn't kept from the lion's den; rather, he was protected once he was already inside. So, I will continue to petition the Lord on behalf of my friends and others I love, but I will not live in fear or worry. I try to think about what I would do for my own children. Even when they're being the worst possible version of themselves, there's nothing I wouldn't do for them. So even though I can't come close to deserving anything from my Heavenly Father, I know there's nothing He won't do for me, especially carrying my burdens.

Day 339

"Cast your cares on the Lord and he will sustain you; he will never let the righteous be shaken."
Psalms 55:22

Su·stain: verb - strengthen or support physically or mentally

That word has been on constant repeat in my heart. My God will sustain me. When I think of all the burdens others carry and the ones I try so hard to release to Him, I am reminded of His promises. I have not felt very good for over a week now, since last Monday's vomiting episode. The nausea and weak stomach are a constant, not nearly as bad as I've had before, but still just nagging at me. I can't seem to build up much stamina either. I wear down so quickly. The last several days, I've pushed myself to do a lot, and now I'm paying for it.

Day 353

"Let the peace of Christ rule in your hearts, since as members of one body you were called to peace. And be thankful. Let the message of Christ dwell among you richly as you teach and admonish one another with all wisdom through psalms, hymns, and songs from the Spirit, singing to God with gratitude in your hearts. And whatever you do, whether in word or deed, do it all in the name of the Lord Jesus, giving thanks to God the Father through him."
Colossians 3:15-17

It's quickly approaching the one-year mark of the day my world was sent spinning. I've gone back to my journal countless times to re-read about God's incredible goodness. I'm so thankful for the encouragement He has given me that is timeless. I can get through any day, especially today. My heart will be filled with praise and gratitude for all He has done and for what He will always do for me. I have almost forgotten I'm #godsfave

Day 365

"Rejoice in the Lord always. I will say it again: Rejoice!
Let your gentleness be evident to all. The Lord is near. Do
not be anxious about anything, but in every situation,
by prayer and petition, with thanksgiving, present your
requests to God. And the peace of God, which transcends
all understanding, will guard your hearts and your minds
in Christ Jesus. Finally, brothers and sisters, whatever is
true, whatever is noble, whatever is right, whatever is pure,
whatever is lovely, whatever is admirable—if anything
is excellent or praiseworthy—think about such things.
Whatever you have learned or received or heard from me,
or seen in me—put it into practice. And the God of peace
will be with you. I rejoiced greatly in the Lord that at
last you renewed your concern for me. Indeed, you were
concerned, but you had no opportunity to show it. I am
not saying this because I am in need, for I have learned
to be content whatever the circumstances. I know what it
is to be in need, and I know what it is to have plenty. I
have learned the secret of being content in any and every
situation, whether well fed or hungry, whether living
in plenty or in want. I can do all this through him who
gives me strength. And my God will meet all your needs
according to the riches of his glory in Christ Jesus."
Philippians 4:4-13, 19

It has been exactly one year. When I heard the words "You have cancer," I had no idea what lay ahead of me. I was scared of what I didn't know. The only thing I was certain of was that the Lord would take care of me. I've had days when I thought my world was over and clearly it wasn't. Every time I wanted to give up or give in, somehow, I came through it.

I don't know what the future holds for me or my family, but I can say with every confidence it will be ok. Even if it wasn't God's plan to heal me, it would still be ok. Sad. But ok. Life goes on even when we think we can't take one more thing, but I've learned that we can, and we do, because of God's grace. When we are weak, he is strong. There will be more challenging days in my future when I'll feel like I'm going to break, but I won't. I will get through whatever it is. And when those times come, I hope I can remember all the times He brought me through before.

I am always reminded of Philippians 4: God is near. Give all your worries to Him, and He will give you peace that passes understanding and supply all of our needs. These are not just words to me; I have lived these truths. They live in my heart and come to mind when I need them most. I'm forever grateful for the ol' Baptist Bible drill competition from my childhood, which branded scripture on my heart.

Day 409

"When I am afraid, I put my trust in you."
Psalm 56:3

It happened—the most incredible thing happened. I got a publishing contract. I've been walking on air all day—more like walking in a state of shock and awe at how amazing God is.

Day 457

*"What, then, shall we say in response to these things? If
God is for us, who can be against us?"*
Romans 8:31

I sang my Father's praises the whole way home from an unexpected visit to Moffitt. Not because I'm having a good day, but quite the
opposite, in fact. I'm no stranger to His goodness and His ability to
turn molehills into majestic mountains. He works all things for my
good because He loves me. My left implant, the non-cancer boob,
has formed an abscess. It's not too common, but it does happen since
there is no barrier between the implant and my epidermis. It's painful.
Doc says It looks like I will be having surgery next week, which may
disrupt many fun events I have coming up. I'm not happy about it
at all. I was just getting back into a routine and feeling like I could
put this all behind me, and focus on *You Don't Need Headlights to
Shine*, which is turning out to be more than I could've ever dreamed
#Godsfave

So, leaving Moffitt, I felt overwhelmed once again; my plans, my
work schedule, and my finances were up in the air. But what have I
learned in all of this? My God has never left me. I never had a bill
go unpaid. I never missed an opportunity to have fun. And me and
Jesus will be thick as thieves once again. I cry because I'm mad at the
disturbance, but really, what I've learned is so amazing. I believe that
the forces of evil can only react to what God has already done. So,
until God does something in the spiritual realm, I believe evil doesn't
interfere. I know God is doing big things in my life. I can't wait. I'm
excited for it. Bring it on! A song came on as I drove home, "Not
today, Satan," and even though I didn't know the words, I learned the
hook real quick. I sang not today, Satan. Because my King has already
gone before me on this, so we'll play a little hopscotch with the things

DAY 460

My story has become a tale of two titties
I have no idea why I thought I could finally put all of this
behind me and focus on real life again...

My doctor said to come immediately
to the ER and he worked me into his schedule last night...

I can potentially have minor surgeries for years to come...

he throws my way but my pathway has already been made and I ain't
leavin it.

"But you are a chosen people, a royal priesthood, a holy nation, God's special possession, that you may declare the praises of him who called you out of darkness into his wonderful light. Once you were not a people, but now you are the people of God; once you had not received mercy, but now you have received mercy."
1 Peter 2:9-10

My story has become a tale of two titties. I have no idea why I thought I could finally put all of this behind me and focus on real life again. With the release of *You Don't Need Headlights to Shine* coming soon, there's so much to be done, and it's happening fast. I could focus on my family and getting back to the salon. It's been great! But whatever God is doing with *You Don't Need Headlights to Shine* is making the forces of evil work over time. But I'll overcome any stones or boulders that come my way because God has already walked my path.

Last week I noticed the scar on my left (non-cancer) boob was peeling a little. I figured it was because I had stopped using my oils and scar creams. It's been over a year now, so I didn't think I needed to keep applying. A few days later, my scar was darker. I took a picture. Every day after that, it was darker and darker, and the skin was thinner and thinner until I knew something wasn't right. I sent my plastic surgeon's nurse a picture. She was concerned that my implant was exposing itself through the thin skin. So, we scheduled surgery for the following week, but my skin didn't make it that long.

Yesterday morning, my bra was wet from the abscess opening in my skin, which I'm told can lead to infection. My doctor said to come immediately to the ER, and he worked me into his schedule last night. There are so many factors that went into this happening. It's no one's fault; it's just part of the cancer life. I can potentially have minor surgeries for years to come. This time, it just happened to be emergent, and I was not prepared. I've been aggravated about it throwing a wrench back into my life. But the things I know for sure are this: God is never surprised. He has already gone before me and has a plan. I don't need to worry about anything. I can be mad, sad, and frustrated. But I cannot worry. It's being handled, like all the things. He has shown me over and over through this process that He never fails. He has proven that I am His favorite. So, I will act like it. I will take all the proof He's given me over the last 460 days and I will meditate on that.

Day 466

"Surely he took up our pain and bore our suffering, yet we considered him punished by God, stricken by him, and afflicted."
Isaiah 53:4

After my emergency surgery six days ago to repair the abscess, the nurse informed me that they cultured the pocket and did not find any infection. But I know from seventh-grade science class that you put a culture in a petri dish to see if it grows over a number of days. And, of course, I like to keep things spicy, so when I went for my post-op appointment yesterday, the doctor informed me that, in fact, the culture had grown. It had grown yeast. It had probably been growing since my initial mastectomy over one year ago, causing the abscess. What doc? I say. Am I some kind of bread factory now? Am I supposed to feed the 5000 with five little loaves like the story from the Bible? Doc quickly named me "Panera Bread," and at my next visit, I will bring him a fresh loaf, not from my yeast, of course, from the store. But really, does this ever end? Surgery is becoming my new hobby.

Day 471

As for me, I will always have hope; I will praise you more and more.
Psalm 71:14

Since having emergency surgery to repair my abscess, everything is healing nicely. I can see why so many women opt out of reconstructive surgeries or give up. I never thought after a year that something like this could happen. I feel hindered in my progress. All the antibiotics I'm on from the infection make me feel sickly and dizzy. I had come so far only to feel like I was starting over again. I know there's a bigger plan, and I trust it. I just wish it didn't involve recovery.

The recovery time has really been helpful as far as working on *You Don't Need Headlights to Shine*. My editor and I (I have my very own editor; it's insane) have been able to get so much accomplished. If I had been working these last weeks, we would have never gotten through the first round of editing. I had no idea what it actually took to get a book out into the world. I'll never look at a book the same way again.

Day 472

When I woke up this morning, my pajama top was wet. Before I could even look to see what I was dealing with, my entire body went into a state of panic. My mind racing. I felt my chin start to quiver. I took a deep breath. Texted my nurse and waited for her to call. Fluid is leaking out of my newly repaired breast, right through the stitches. I sent her a picture, which she relayed to the on-call surgeon since my surgeon is on vacation this week.

I'm on my way back to the emergency room. Even though I sent pictures and video of it actively leaking, the doctors like to put their own eyes on it. She said to pack an overnight bag just in case they decide to admit me for antibiotics overnight and head straight to the ER.

I'm teary. But I'm not sure how I feel exactly. I'm disappointed that I had to cancel lunch with two girlfriends today. I'm anxious to see what the doctor decides. I'm in shock, maybe? Numb? I try not to let myself think of all the what-ifs. My nurse did use the words "hoping to salvage your breast." Skin can only handle so much. My entire body has been through so much in the last 472 days. Right now, I'm not going to overthink or analyze. I've been in this state of emotion many times before on this journey. I feel shaky on the inside, but on the outside, I become focused on the task. Phone calls. Packing. Preparing. Once I know exactly what's ahead, then I can break down.

I'm all checked into the ER. I've been triaged. As I sit and wait, I look out onto the beautiful ocean. The water is calm on the surface. Much like I am right now. And even though deep down I am unsure,

I am not troubled. I have that weird sense of peace again and know my Father is with me. My story is not over. Every time I tell a friend about a new development, they say, "Another chapter for *You Don't Need Headlights to Shine*"! And that may be what all this is for. Another bump, another chapter, another person this could help. Another reminder for myself to surrender everything to God.

Doc is admitting me. Infectious disease docs are involved now. Nothing by mouth after midnight in case surgery is needed. I've reached out to my praying people. The realization that I could lose my breast completely is weighing very heavily on me right now. I do not want that to be how my story goes. At all. I know I didn't want cancer either, and I ended up being grateful that it chose me. But this possibility.... I'm just not even considering it.

Day 473

*"Therefore, my dear brothers and sisters, stand firm. Let
nothing move you. Always give yourselves fully to the work
of the Lord, because you know that your labor in the
Lord is not in vain."*
1 Corinthians 15:58

I was admitted overnight in hopes that IV antibiotics would clear
up any remaining infection. I dozed off and on with the usual hospital interruptions. My brain has been paralyzed when it comes to any
thoughts of surgery or the dreadful possibilities that could come with
that.

Just before dawn, after a pretty restless night, my plastics team
came in to see me. It looks like I'll be headed to the OR later today
after all. The plan is to clean out the infection and replace the implant
with a smaller one to give my skin a better chance of healing. I'm not
going to think about that right now. My stomach's growling so loud
I can't concentrate anyway. Yesterday, I was so anxious and nauseated
that I could only manage to get down a granola bar. And now I will
have to go without food all day today.

My sweet-as-pie nurse and I have become besties. In 12 hours,
we've managed to get into the nitty gritty conversations of life. She
just came in to say goodbye. Her shift is ending. And she spoke words
over me that I felt came straight from Jesus. She used specific wording
that I use when I pray. She spoke those same words back to me out
loud. As I stared at her in amazement, I got emotional. Hearing those
words of healing and encouragement affirmed to me that I will be ok.
This is another part of my journey. I know what to do. I'm familiar
with all the feelings that come with this process and I know Jesus is
with me.

436 days ago, I had a mastectomy and implants put in. I knew I
was so fortunate that it worked out that way because so many prob-

lems can occur. I thought I was out of danger. I thought I could put that part of the journey far behind me. The plastics team informed me today that they decided it's best to remove the implant and not replace it. At least until it heals completely. This has shaken me. More so than the cancer diagnosis. I don't want to even think the words, much less type them. Doc used words like "prosthetic" and phrases like "we'll try to replace the implant in the future." She said it was ok to be mad or upset that my feelings were valid. But it's more important for me to be 100% well. She's right. But I don't want to hear that. Every person saying these things to me has two titties! I'm mad at God right now. And I told Him so. I thought I was your favorite! So why is this part of my journey??? He reminded me that I surrendered my whole self to be used for Him. And I did. I'm just gonna be mad about it for a little bit.

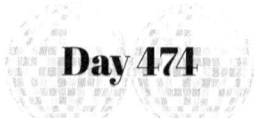

Day 474

*"Let the morning bring me word of your unfailing love, for
I have put my trust in you. Show me the way I should go,
for to you I entrust my life."*
Psalm 143:8

Between the anesthesia and the shock of it all, I'm not sure what
I wrote yesterday. But today is much better for me mentally. I'm
clear-headed even though I'm still sleepy.

I understand the importance of removing the implant for my
health, and I realize that these things can and do happen. But after
so long, I thought I was out of the woods. After looking somewhat
normal, even without nipples, I was beginning to like myself again.
My hair is growing into a cute curly bob, and my clothes are fitting
nicely. I even ordered a new bathing suit for our summer beach trip.
A prosthetic breast doesn't align with the plans I made.

I surrendered early on in this journey to be used by God in whatever way He could use me the most to shine the spotlight on Him.
Now he has two spotlights without any headlights, but they will still
shine bright!

A lady came in to clean up my room. She was filled with joy and
spoke words of healing over me. I told her I was a bit discouraged
about losing my boob, and boy, did she remind me how blessed I still
am to be here. Thank God she was bold in her faith to me. We even
laughed and made jokes that I should get half a refund for my titty
that was removed. I know she was here to clean my room, but she was
sent to my room specifically from Jesus. So, I could hear out loud how
blessed I really am.

Day 475

"I waited patiently for the Lord; He turned to me and heard my cry. He lifted me out of the slimy pit, out of the mud and mire; He set my feet on a rock and gave me a firm place to stand."
Psalm 40:1-2

Think of the oldest, wrinkliest, toothless man you have ever seen. That's what my non-boob looks like. A drawn-in, toothless, haggard mouth. I finally saw it today with no bandages or tape. I got to take a glorious shower, and so all of the band-aids had to come off. I was oddly unaffected and deeply affected at the same time. I was sad, but I also knew it was temporary. I'm either at peace or in shock. For a lot of women, this is their reality forever. I'm praying that I will get another chance to replace the implant and also that SpongeBlob continues to behave so, I can keep him just like he is.

My pity party has significantly decreased since I originally found out they'd take my implant and not replace it. I'm still sad about my beach vacation and all the outfits I have that don't require a bra. I have to reconfigure a prosthetic into all of them now—even my bathing suit. But I'm alive! And I get to continue living because I am healed from cancer. For some reason, my story is not finished being told.

Day 476

"He put a new song in my mouth, a hymn of praise to our God. Many will see and fear the Lord and put their trust in Him."
Psalm 40:3

I'm numb. I realize I should be having all sorts of emotions at this point, but I'm almost emotionless. I have no idea what's going on. It's like there's no concept of time. I'm just existing. I'm interacting with others normally and they ask how I am. Blank. Nothing comes to mind. It's different than before when I was diagnosed. That was like an out-of-body experience. I am very much in my body, present in mind. When the doctor told me they would most definitely be taking my left breast and not reconstructing it, I remember thinking this is not what I wanted. I remember telling myself I could fall apart when she left the hospital room. She even told me I was justified in doing so. She said to let it all out that it was normal. And when she left the room, nothing. It wasn't until I was being wheeled into the OR and the surgeon explained it could be 6-9 months or longer that I could be without a breast that I finally shed a tear. How could this be happening an entire year after I've had reconstructive surgery? I've been with Tweedle D and DD for a year!!! They have been fine! Why now? We were a team. We came through this together. All this time, with no bra, I'm finally completely used to not having nipples! We are normal again! What's the point of this part of the story?

I'm clearly angry. Writing this has stirred emotion in me. I am pissed. I know all of the things about how it's more important to be healthy and all that crap. I know God is with me, and He doesn't want this for me either, but He'll use it for good. I. Know. All. This. But I don't like it. I had moved on from cancer. I had moved on from identifying with that in my daily life. I was working on my book and looking forward to helping others with my story. I was working an almost normal schedule. I was making money again. I was involved with my kids' daily lives again. I was happy.

What is this feeling? Disappointment? Denial? Anger? Sadness? None of these words seem to describe it. Or maybe all of them do. I want to step outside of my own reality just for a minute and clear my thoughts. I want to go back to Sponge Blob being my biggest problem.

My follow-up appointment is in three more days. I think I'm barely hanging on to see what Doc says then. He was on vacation when all of this happened, so maybe I'm hoping he'll swoop in and save the day by giving me the news I want to hear. Until then, I'll get some good rest. Maybe things will look better in the morning.

Day 477

"Restore to me the joy of your salvation and grant me a willing spirit, to sustain me."
Psalm 51:12

I am reminded that Jesus restores me. I am walking around right now with one nippleless breast and one flat tire, an old man-looking blob, but Jesus is not finished with me, physically or spiritually. I know when I look back on this, I will not have traded it because whatever God has in store for me is so much better. I got comfortable and was making my own plans again. I thought I had things figured out. Get back to the salon, work on my book and be a mom again. The feeling of having the rug pulled from under my feet is here again. I know better than to try and push my own agenda. I've got to let God have total control. And I feel like I have. As much as I know how to. I think I'm not understanding what exactly I am supposed to be doing. I'm anxious to get back to my job because that's what I am supposed to do, right? I can't imagine that I shouldn't aim to get back into the salon. Part of my identity is being a stylist and I'm just programmed to get back to it. But what if God's plan for me isn't that? He would really have to spell it out for me at that point. Like huge letters in the sky. Even then, Chad would have to be a witness to it because he sure doesn't think that it's God's plan for me not to work.

My faith is solid. I have never thought for a second that I don't need it or could turn away from it. I talk to God very raw these days. I lash out, roll my eyes, and look up in disgust. He knows my deepest, most inner thoughts anyway. I might as well be honest outwardly about it. And He is unfazed. He is not surprised this happened and He is not surprised at my reaction. He is still here with loving open arms. Psalm 103 was written by David in his midst of turmoil. It's a psalm of praise. I read it in many different translations. I will praise my Father because He is always good even when my situation is not good.

One of the Pastors I follow was talking about the trials of life. He said the way we handle trials is an example to someone else. I am a witness to what God is doing in my life. And that may make someone else more bold in their own faith. It may give them courage in their own battle. Keeping my eyes on the Lord has not only kept me from experiencing so much anguish, but it could also inspire someone else to do the same in their struggle.

I still fail to see how in the world God can use me or why he would choose me. I am the farthest from being worthy. I know we don't need to be worthy for him to use us. We never could be good enough on our own merit. But that's the beauty of my situation. In my flawed state He will shine brighter than I could've ever dreamed through this mess of a chest. I have this feeling that something huge is on the horizon. I reminded him (myself) that I am a blank canvas. I surrendered control, and He can paint me any way He chooses. I fully trust that whatever His will for my life is, it's way better than the plan I could invent.

*"Start children off on the way they should go, and even
when they are old they will not turn from it."*
Proverbs 22:6

For me, the challenges of motherhood are so much greater than all this cancer stuff. I think back to diagnosis, treatment, hair loss, surgeries and now the loss of a breast, and it all seems so much easier to deal with than raising teenagers. Partly because all of those things were mine to bear. When your child has a problem or a hurt, you cannot take it from them. You can only give advice and pray and guide them from experience. If I could just take their hurts as my own, it would be so much better. Because I could deal with it. I could fix it. And if it isn't fixable I could carry it. Just like all this cancer stuff. I'm healed from cancer but bear the side effects from the whole process, and while it hasn't been a dream, I am getting through it. Most days are good days. I can't handle not being able to fix things for my girls. I've prayed every prayer I can muster. I've asked God to give me their struggles for myself.

But isn't that how God feels about us? He says to hand over all of our burdens for him to carry and yet we don't. I don't know why some days are so hard and I know they'll get past it, normal growing pains. I sent us all to bed for the night because everything looks better after a good night's sleep and I say one last prayer, begging God to help me get through the hardest job on earth.

Day 479

My plastic surgeon is back from vacation and got to see my non-titty for the first time. He was sad. He said this wasn't supposed to happen. It was very validating to hear him say what I was thinking. But we all (in the cancer business) know things like this happen. I just thought after an entire year, I could take a sigh of relief. Now, I've learned that anything is possible. Doc removed my drain - Praise the Lord - and said that he would remove my stitches in two weeks. Then came the big question.

When can Humpty Dumpty be put back together again?

Without hesitation, he said I would be ready in six months.

I can do this. I can handle six months. In the last week living with one boob, it has been the punch line for any and every joke. I've been ok with it because I had hoped to be whole again. And now that I'm sure of that, I really am fine. I'll continue to joke about my flat tire, old man without teeth looking titty. I need to name it. Pepaw or grandpappy. When it's staring back at me in the mirror, I can imagine it saying, "Heh, sonny-boy? Did u say sumthn?" Just like a little ol' toothless grandpa.

I left the doctor's office with more of a pep in my step and headed to the cancer clinic to pick up my soft prosthetic. Some genius invented these incredibly soft, light-as-air "pillow" prosthetics that are safe to wear immediately after surgery, even with a drain or stitches. I chose the large-size soft prosthetic package. It comes with a camisole and soft rounds of Velcro right inside, and voila. You have boobs again! But I didn't try them on in the clinic. I grabbed the package, thanked the nurse and went to my car.

Driving home, I kept glancing over at the package of boobies in the passenger seat. Stopped at a traffic light, I finally reached over and tore into the bag. I pull out the softest material in the world. Round little pockets filled with cottony stuffing. The most simple invention ever. Every woman in the world invented this when they were in the fifth grade using socks. We all stuffed our bras! Unless you were one of those who blossomed super early.

I immediately put the soft round pillow down my shirt. It's huge in comparison to Sponge Blob! So, I yank it out and start pulling out stuffing! By now traffic is flowing again and I'm unstuffing and restuffing and smooshing the pillow to get it the same size as my other boob. The weather was so nice I had the sunroof open, and stuffing started flying around the car in a whirlwind right out of the sunroof. I panicked for a second! Wait! That's my boob! I might need that! Then I remembered they came as a pair and I had another boob in the passenger seat just in case I took out too much stuffing. I continue to stuff and adjust for several miles in my own little world. Completely oblivious of how I must've looked to passersby. I have no idea what snapped me out of my obsession with getting it just right. I think I finally had the right amount, patted it down and adjusted my seatbelt over it.

Much better! I feel balanced now. It's not so bad. My clothes fit how they should. I can live with Pepaw for 6 months or so. I will be ok.

Day 481

"They are like a man building a house, who dug down deep and laid the foundation on rock. When a flood came, the torrent struck that house but could not shake it, because it was well built."
Luke 6:48

At this point in my journey, I look back and see that Jesus has been my rock. So many times, when I thought I would crumble for sure, I didn't. I have Jesus as my firm foundation. In the Bible, there's a parable about a man who builds his house on the sand and a man who builds his house on solid rock. The house built on sand crumbles from the tiniest storm. The man who built his house on the rock stood firm even through a monstrous storm. I can't say enough how thankful I am that I have built my faith on solid rock. Each time in my life, in this journey, when one more problem would pile on, I would think this is it. I'll collapse this time. I'm not gonna make it. I can't take one more thing. I made it through because of my faith. I've been asked so many times why I wasn't freaking out. Was I in denial about the things I was going through? I don't think so. I think it's because deep down, I know the Author of my life. He gives me inexplicable peace in the middle of monstrous storms.

Day 482

*"For God so loved the world that he gave his one and only
Son, that whoever believes in him shall not perish but have
eternal life."*
John 3:16

I never intended to write about my faith so much, but at this
point, if you're still reading, you've seen the escalation coming. I feel
God is preparing me to share my story on a bigger scale than I am
comfortable with. I'm facing challenges that I never thought would
come, and He is using them to get me ready. I have no idea what is
ahead for me or for *You Don't Need Headlights to Shine*. But I do not
doubt that He has a plan for both. I wasn't ready for whatever was
coming, and because of this setback, losing my left breast, it's become
clear that I have to use it as another opportunity to learn and grow.
There is someone out there, I believe, that I can help by being bold
in my faith. God has them in mind. He is using this story to get their
attention. It could be you, the reader, right now. God has tried to get
your attention to let you know how much He loves you and He would
do anything for you, including sending his innocent son as a sacrifice. I'm no Bible scholar or religion expert. What I have is first-hand
experience of the true love of God. And He will fight to have your
love in return. All I ever did was surrender control of my life into His
hands. I didn't wait until I was cleaned up or perfect. I surrendered in
the midst of my mess. I said God you made me, I know you love me,
so help me. And He has and He always will. My heart wants every
person in the world to have this experience for themselves. It is so
comforting to know I am never alone in any situation. I believe God
will chase you and never stop, but sometimes we can be so caught up
in ourselves that we don't realize it.

There's a verse in the Bible that says, "Be still. And know that I
am God." It means to literally stop, be quiet, meditate, whatever is

comfortable for you. Sit in the quietness, call on Him and He will answer you. God is Love. If you accept His love, I promise you will never regret it.

Day 483

"Sing for joy to God our strength; shout aloud to the God of Jacob!"
Psalm 81:1

I'm tired of doing hard things. I've grown weary. I have this feeling of nothingness. I have filled my days with friends and activities, so from the outside, I seem so normal I have even fooled myself. It's been 10 days since my latest surgery and 24 days since the first surgery when this fiasco started up again. I have been the ideal patient, resting and recouping because everyone is so worried I'll overdo it. I physically feel fine, zero pain or discomfort. I think all the nerves have been severed so many times now that I truly have no sense of feeling. And since I'm on a break from the Dragon, I don't have to go to the "gym" unexpectedly and my joints are feeling better. My struggle is inward. I'm so good at distracting myself that I haven't really sat alone with my thoughts. I'm in a tough season of life right now. I'm trying to balance so many things between my health, the girls, work and this book. But I'm afraid of what will happen if I slow down. It's like I'm waiting for the other shoe to drop. And I'm not a doomsday kinda person. I keep running (not physically ever) and going, doing, and planning because if I stop....what? I don't know. I'm scared to go there in my thoughts. I don't like this. I don't want to do difficult anymore. I need a break. I want a vacation from being me, even if it's just a minute. I feel terrible thinking this because there are far worse situations than mine. But I only live my reality. And sometimes it gets to be too much.

Day 484

"Come to me, all you who are weary and burdened, and I will give you rest."
Matthew 11:28

I'm in a foul mood today. I have such little tolerance for even minute things. My insides feel jittery. I think it's partly because I started back to work today and all of the things going on in my life are mounting up. But instead of me focusing on them, I have to focus on my clients. Which is a good distraction, but problems loom over me.

I'm carrying burdens for my girls that I can't seem to put down. I go back and forth between vengefulness and letting God have the final say. I'm just now to the point in my life where I have learned that letting God handle when we feel we've been wronged turns out far better than anything I could do. Yet I fight the urge to defend the truth. I know the right thing to do, and if the offense had been toward me, I could let it go. There's just something feral inside of me when it comes to protecting my kids.

And Pepaw. Do I need to explain? There is such a range of emotions that come with cancer-related issues. It seems a lifetime ago when I was diagnosed, yet I can conjure up the emotions of that day. By now, I've been up and down over and over, and I'm no stranger to this ride. In these low moments, I try my best to learn from them and remind myself of all the things I've learned along the way. I know that before long, things will be up again, and this will be behind me. I can't wait for that day.

Day 487

*"Let us then approach God's throne of grace with
confidence, so that we may receive mercy and find grace to
help us in our time of need."*
Hebrews 4:16

I ended an extremely busy work week on a good note. I am still struggling with my inner demons, but my brothers and I were under the same roof once again. It's been over a decade since we were all together. We joked and laughed at old stories and roasted Mom and Dad. That's one thing all three of us can always come together about. We love making fun of mom and dad. And my parents are pretty good sports about it. I'm grateful for this time together. I don't know how many more moments like this we will have, but I will always have the memory of tonight.

All of the heaviness from earlier this week has lifted some. I cannot see the bigger picture but God's plan is always better. Some problems are just harder for me to relinquish. I've been wallowing for some time now and I'm getting sick of myself. I'm thinking there has to be a breakthrough on the horizon.

Day 488

"But as for me, I watch in hope for the Lord , I wait for God my Savior; my God will hear me. Do not gloat over me, my enemy! Though I have fallen, I will rise. Though I sit in darkness, the Lord will be my light."
Micah 7:7-8

Once you hit bottom there's only one direction to go next. I thought many times during this cancer experience that I had hit rock bottom, only to find out that it wasn't the bottom. But once Pepaw entered the story stage left, I reached my breaking point. Initially I tried to ignore my reality, and that worked for a while. Then, I confronted my situation and lashed out at God. Now I am focused on rising to the occasion. Like so many other times on this voyage, I came across Scripture that gave me comfort in God's unfailing word. Opening my Bible app and reading this verse validated how I've been feeling. But soon, I will rise again.

Day 490

The Lord will fight for you; you need only to be still.
Exodus 14:14

Has God changed his mind about using me to help others? We've been playing the silent game again, but I'm hopeful things are about to change. I don't feel as defeated today, and so many people I love have bigger struggles than a missing boob. I know so many battling very difficult prognoses, divorce and financial issues that I can't be upset about Pepaw anymore. I've been so focused on praying for others the last few days that it has helped me to see the bigger picture. I want healing for those I love. I want to give them the hope I have. I want to give them the healing I've experienced. I want them to have the peace I've known. I want to physically share all the good stuff. I have to be thankful for my struggles because, without them, there would be no growth. I am reminded of King David. He was anointed to be king as a young man, a shepherd boy, but did not become king for many years later. In between the waiting period, he encountered so many obstacles that helped him grow so that he could one day rule. I am not David by any stretch of the imagination, but I know God is using my struggle with a purpose in mind. While I wait for Him to reveal my next step, I have to remain faithful.

Day 491

"Restore to me the joy of your salvation and grant me a
willing spirit, to sustain me."
Psalm 51:12

I am out of the darkness and I'm feeling more like myself again. Talking things through with my clients helps more than I realized. Telling the story over and over about my last two hospital stays makes it more like a story I'm telling about someone else, and at the end of the day, I feel cleansed from baring my soul all day. I'm honest about the low points and about how I was so angry that this was happening more than a year later. No one is shocked, and they agree they'd feel the same way. And, of course, to keep it light and fluffy, I tell them about Pepaw. In the end I'm thankful that even Pepaw won't be sticking around too long. It's important for me to remain hopeful, even at my lowest moments. Losing hope leads to a lack of faith, and a lack of faith leads to places I don't want to go. I can't let my emotions dictate how I react when I'm discouraged. Even though I did not feel grateful or happy or peaceful I made myself practice thankfulness. And eventually, it became my true feelings. It's a decision I made long ago when I chose to have a relationship with Jesus. I know he has never left me, even when I feel he's silent. I remember all the times before when He's rescued me, and that's what I dwell on until he pulls me out of despair again.

Day 492

"In their hearts humans plan their course,
but the Lord establishes their steps."
Proverbs 16:9

My heart is so full. Lately I have felt so defeated when it comes to parenting. I think maybe a sign of good parenting is that you never quite feel like you're doing it right. No one does exactly, but the fact that you're concerned about it means you care. But every once in a while, you get that sign of reassurance that you are doing something right. Today was one of those days. We can tell our children things until we are blue in the face, but until they experience it for themselves, it doesn't stick. And sometimes they will do greater things than you even prayed for and those are the moments when I feel my heart will explode with joy. We can make all the plans in the world for ourselves and our kids, but Proverbs 16 says the Lord determines our steps. That means His ways are better than any plan we can devise. So even when we are disappointed with the way things are going that doesn't mean it's wrong or it won't turn out well. I can see that I still have so much more I need to trust God with. I knew there was something better just around the corner. I'm so glad I held on.

Day 493

Pepaw's stitches are out! It wasn't a very pleasant feeling, even though I'm mostly numb. The resident carefully tugged and snipped at the 5-inch incision. Doc said everything has healed nicely and the skin looks healthy. So, of course, I was ready to set a date for my reconstruction surgery because I'm a planner, and I'd really like to have a day set to look forward to. He was very nonchalant about it. He said let's wait and have another follow-up before we book so far into the future. What?? Way to rub it in, Doc! I know six months is far away. It's a long time to live with Pepaw. I needed him to be more enthusiastic about repairing me. I will go back in about three months and we'll take it from there. It's just that I live my life on a daily planner, scheduling clients, trips, doctors' appointments, dinners, lunches, the kids activities. I'd love to see reconstructive surgery on the docket. It will come in time. I'm just not a patient person.

Two more friends of mine were diagnosed with cancer today. They both thought to call me soon after they found out. They were both stunned. I remember that feeling all too well. I tried my best to be careful with my words, even though they welcomed any advice I could offer. People mean well, but they don't always know what to say. And until you are facing something like cancer, you don't know what you don't like to hear either. I get so irritated at the silliest things people say sometimes, and I'm sure they are things I used to say to others before I was diagnosed. I mainly told my friends the facts and passed along doctor information and reassured them they had so much support. But it's not really a time for words of comfort. You're in such a state of shock that you can't wrap your head around the fact that it's happening and you just want to keep pushing through to the next step and the next. I didn't want to hear how I would kick cancer's ass or I would get through it or my diagnosis was one of the better ones to have. I just needed information and how to get time to move faster. These two friends make 18 total that I personally know who are fighting some form of cancer. My prayer list sadly continues to grow. One more reason I'd love to get *You Don't Need Headlights to Shine* out into the world and hopefully help encourage these friends and so many more.

Day 497

"Truly He is my rock and my salvation; He is my fortress, I will not be shaken."
Psalm 62:6

I had my appointment at the prosthetic boutique today. The word boutique describes it exactly. I felt like a princess except for the missing boob. The women greeted me with such kindness as do all Moffitt employees. I was led to a private dressing room that was decorated in soft shades of pink. A beautiful floral rug covered the floor; in the corner was a set of cozy chairs and a floor-length mirror. Bras upon bras lined the walls and shelves. All are neatly color-coordinated. There were cubbies filled with every size prosthetic breast imaginable. It looked like chicken cutlets at a meat market, but in the prettiest setting, of course.

The two women (one was in training) began by giving me a top that opened in the front and offered to leave the room while I changed. Aren't they about to see me in all my glory? I told them at this point I had zero modesty left as I removed my top and said let's get this party started. I imagine for some women, this is very emotional, and they were giving me respect. But they don't know how crazy I am and that I'm ready to cover up Pepaw as soon as possible. They began measuring me much like a normal bra fitting, asking questions about my previous bra size and what types of bras I prefer. She began pulling different styles of bras from the rack and then helped me try them on. She fastened and tightened or loosened the straps while we gazed in the mirror to see the outcome. Then came the chicken cutlets. All shapes and sizes. Full prosthetic, partial prosthetic, waterproof, active lifestyle and so on. Thank God these women know their stuff because I wouldn't have known where to start.

One hour and $500 later, I left with four bras and two prosthetics, all beautifully packaged in pink tissue paper. I will have to submit the paperwork, which they provided me with, to my insurance company for reimbursement. Overall, it was a very pleasant experience, but I hope to never go back. This should last me until I have Pepaw reconstructed, and hopefully, I can put this part of my journey behind me for good.

Day 498

*"I will give you a new heart and put a new spirit in you;
I will remove from you your heart of stone and give you a
heart of flesh."*
Ezekiel 36:26

Chad and I are watching a series called The Chosen. It depicts the life of Jesus' ministry and his disciples. The series shows the disciples as real, ordinary people with jobs, families and major character flaws. Growing up hearing about all of the miracles Jesus performed, I never gave thought to what his followers must've gone through at the time. None of them were worthy enough to be chosen. Jesus knew Judas would go on to betray him for 30 pieces of silver, yet he was a disciple. Matthew, the tax collector, was despised by everyone, but Jesus welcomed him into his inner circle. The point is that no one is worthy enough. But Jesus doesn't ask us to be. He loves us where we are at this very moment. All he asks is that we follow him. Long ago, on this cancer journey, my heart changed. I chose to follow Jesus in a way I had never done before. I surrendered myself in the middle of a disaster wholeheartedly to be an example of faith. I pray every day that I am able to do justice to the job he has called me to do. The TV series has shown me that even though the chosen were eyewitnesses to the miracles he performed, they still had doubts and fears of their own to contend with. The struggles of Life still got in the way of how they wanted to follow Jesus. I know every time I am faced with a new challenge, I have to stay focused on Jesus and everything else will fall into place.

Day 499

Surely, Lord, you bless the righteous; you surround them
with your favor as with a shield.
Psalm 5:12

It's been almost two weeks since I started taking the Dragon again. I've spent the better part of the last two days in the "gym." I have mouth and nose sores, and I'm easily fatigued. But I will get back into a rhythm soon so that I can have more predictable visits to the gym.

My prosthetic and special bras are comfortable and I almost forget about Pepaw hiding out underneath. As I am slowly getting back to work, all of my clients want to know what's been going on and what led to the last two surgeries. I realized after talking with some of them that there is so much confusion when it comes to a mastectomy with reconstruction. The medical term for my procedure is called a bilateral mastectomy with direct implants. That means I left the hospital with new boobs right away. I never had to go through a waiting period like some women who have reconstructive surgery later on. I compare my mastectomy to carving a pumpkin. The inside of the pumpkin is my breast tissue. The outside of the pumpkin is my skin. The surgeon removed all the breast tissue and left just the skin. The skin was then filled with implants. People get confused when I tell them I no longer have a left breast. They don't understand the process, which technically left me with no breast tissue. Now, I no longer have a left reconstructed breast. There is nothing left but a concave wrinkled scar. Hopefully, my skin is healthy enough to accept a new implant in six months. I really need to wrap my head around the possibility that I may need to go with a smaller size or that I may not be able to do the surgery at all. Right now, the doctor is very positive that things will be able to go back to how they were before, but now I know that's not always the case.

People make comments like they would just cut their boobs off,

DAY 500

I see the light at the end of the tunnel.
I am whole because where I am lacking Jesus
fills in the gaps.

I am at peace now and I'll be fine whatever
comes my way in the future.

or why would you go through all of that, or I just wouldn't do anything. These are comments that get on my nerves, but I know they're
not meant maliciously. You just don't know what you'd do until you're
in that situation. At my age, I feel like I'm too young to go without
breasts if I am able to try. Maybe if I were much older, I wouldn't
mind as much, but I'm not even sure about that. There are plenty of
survivors out there who didn't have a chance to get reconstruction or
they had it and it failed. I owe it to myself to try every option available to me, and writing about it will possibly help someone else in my
shoes. I'm thankful for my sense of humor, especially at this point in
my journey, because laughter sure does help. My friend's husband is
going through chemo right now and today she said if we don't laugh
about it we'd sit around and cry. That's certainly been the case for me.
I'd much rather make fun of Pepaw than dwell on the reality that he

may always be with me, but I'm praying he'll only be in the family for another six months.

"Now all glory to God, who is able, through his mighty power at work within us, to accomplish infinitely more than we might ask or think."
Ephesians 3:20

Boobs are a big part of womanhood. Every set is unique. Big, small, saggy, perky, heavy, light, long, short, teardrop or round shaped. Love 'em or hate 'em they're inevitably part of the territory. Some women live with them and sometimes we have to live without them. But that's the thing….we get to live and that's what's important. Cancer attacked my body, and for a while, I blamed my breasts for betraying me. Cancer was the only one to blame.

I have turned the corner, and Pepaw and I are living in complete harmony. My new bras and prosthetic fit so nicely that I almost forget about him until the end of the day, when I get home and sling my bra off. Then, I am left lopsided in whatever moo-moo I choose to wear around the house. And I don't even care. I feel so at peace. I have no idea what changed, but my heart feels so light.

My curly hair is finally at a length that I enjoy styling and I get lots of compliments. I think it finally looks like a purposeful style instead of the "after chemo, grow out" look. I'm still not sure if the curls will stay but I'm having fun with it for now.

I am mostly accustomed to my medicine regimen, and on rough days, I have learned what works and what doesn't. My energy level is very steady, and I am enjoying life almost the same as I did before cancer. I can go very long stretches without thinking about or even remembering the whole debacle. It's so nice to feel normal again.

Parenting will always ebb and flow, but things are really good at the moment. Summer break is approaching quickly, and it always seems to help knowing we all get a break from the rigorous school days.

I see the light at the end of the tunnel. I am fine. I am happy. I am healed. And if I never get Pepaw fixed I am ok with that too. My family loves me, my friends love me and I finally love me too. Most of all, I know with all certainty Jesus loves me because I have felt his love and experienced his goodness in my life, especially over the last year and a half. I am whole because where I am lacking, Jesus fills in the gaps. I am at peace now and I'll be fine whatever comes my way in the future. He has shown me time and time again that he will never leave me, and he is with me at my lowest the same way he's with me on the mountaintop. My blessings are far too many to count. My faith is deeper than I ever knew, and I am more committed to honoring my Heavenly Father than ever. I can't wait to share my experience in hopes of helping others. I know I will face obstacles in the next chapter of my life, but I am equipped with all the reminders that He is able. So, right now, I plan to have reconstructive surgery in the next six to nine months, but if for some reason that is not in the cards for me, I will be alright. And in the future, if people want to know if Pepaw is still part of the family, all they have to do is ask; after all, I'm an open book.

Now I can look back on it and be thankful for everything I've gone through because I know the whole reason for it all was to share my story with you and to brag about being #Godsfave. But the reality is you're His favorite, too…#weareallgodsfave

The After

When I started this journal, it was for my documentation and quickly turned into God leading my words. The more people I shared it with, the more I was encouraged to keep writing. I feel God laid it on my heart to publish my journal in order to help others. But the closer I got to the one-year mark, I no longer felt that was His plan. I felt that my journal had fulfilled its purpose and helped some others along the way. I prayed many times about what God wanted me to do with *You Don't Need Headlights to Shine*. I looked into publishing from a very surface level, and it seemed out of reach. I had no idea where to start. So, my prayer became, " Lord, if you want this to go any further, you're going to have to drop it in my lap. I will not pursue publishing because it seems too tall of a task." Then, I forgot all about it and put it on the back burner. Until today.

When Presley played sports, we made many friends. In particular, I got very close to one of her teammates' grandmothers. Since I'm an old soul myself, we quickly became besties. Her name is Adina. We shared a love of reading and deep faith. We had lots to talk about and I always looked forward to seeing her. After my diagnosis, we kind of lost touch. Until today. We live so far apart that I never expected to see her in a coffee shop in a town that is 40 minutes from me. It was at our annual Christmas brunch that my friends and I do every year when I spotted her across the restaurant. I beelined toward her and called her name. She turned and recognized me immediately, even with my short hair, squealed my name, and we embraced so hard and so long. It was a hug I had no idea I needed. We fired off questions back and forth. What are you doing here? How are you? Who are you with? She introduced me to her friend Bobbi, who had lost her husband a year ago suddenly, just like Adina had two years prior. They came to the bookstore because Bobbi had written a book about her late husband and she was inquiring about a book signing. I could not believe it. I told her I had written about my cancer journey and thought about publishing, but I gave up because I had no idea where to start. She pulled a flyer out of her pocket with all the information about her publishing firm on it and handed it to me. All three of us were so far from home, standing at this bookstore at the same time. Fate. It also happened to be the one-year anniversary of Bobbi's husband's death and the one-year mark when my doctor called me to confirm my cancer diagnosis. We both had chills the whole time talking about all the coincidences that we knew weren't coincidences. It was the most overwhelming, full-circle moment. I can't describe how full I felt. I could hear God saying I told you so. Look at what I can put together, do you still doubt me now? She told me her publisher is looking for stories of hope to spread light to others.

While my friends waited in the background to find out what all my excitement was about, we continued to share so many moments that we knew were divine appointments. Nothing was a coincidence. Finally, I wished her well at her book signing; we took a picture together and traded numbers and emails. We have already messaged each other, and I've already contacted Lucie, the publisher. So, whether or not anything becomes of this, I have this full circle moment of God proving to me that He will drop things in our lap. All we have to do is ask…

Ten Things I Have Learned from My Journey:

1. God never fails
2. Bad things happen to good people.
3. God turns bad things into good for His glory
4. It. will. be. ok.
5. With Him, I always have hope.
6. His word never returns void
7. I am never alone
8. I know who I can count on
9. Nipples are overrated
10. I am highly favored by God #Godsfave

I am forever grateful for *You Don't Need Headlights to Shine* and the unwavering support I've received from all those that endured this journey with me.

I love you all.

Acknowledgements

To my publisher Lucie for making my dreams come to life. And for your endless support and encouragement.

To my Fairy Godmother, my editor Yvonne. Your ability to create magic is a true gift. I will forever have a little Yvonne on my shoulder speaking encouragement into my ear.

To the EBC for keeping my cup full and overflowing with endless celebrations.

To Janice for your computer knowledge and keeping me out of the dark ages.

To Adina and Bobbi for being at the right place at the right time.

To all my friends for the dinners, cards, texts and support. You'll never know how much it kept me going.

My husband for truly honoring the vow you made to me, for better or worse. I pray I don't have to return the favor anytime soon because I could never measure up.

My beautiful daughters, I hope you know how much I love you and I feel so blessed to be your mama.

My amazing medical professionals at H. Lee Moffitt for unselfishly fighting to find a cure for this dreaded disease.

Shanie for your fighting spirit to help those you love.